A TEACHER'S GUIDE TO
STORYTELLING AT HISTORIC SITES

Eric Maddern

English ☷ Heritage

CONTENTS

**Eric Maddern and
Kathie Prince,
Maiden Castle,
Dorset.**

ENGLISH HERITAGE

ABOUT THIS BOOK

Britain is famous for its past. Millions of people from around the world visit thousands of historic sites in Britain each year. As well as these general visitors numerous groups of local children frequently troop off, clipboard in hand, eager to make something of the ruins of henges, hillforts, castles and abbeys.

Many people want to learn about Britain's fascinating past, some to understand how and why life has changed, others perhaps to profit from it. But most of us would like to be able to imagine what life was really like centuries ago. And often that is the hardest thing to do.

There is a simple and effective way in which ancient places can be brought to life in the imagination, and that is through the telling of stories. Two kinds of stories can help in this task.

First, are the stories that people who lived in these places told each other, usually round the fire, often during the long winter nights - the myths, legends and folktales of the oral tradition. These stories were filtered through generations of storytellers and often contain nuggets of wisdom alongside bizarre characters, magical happenings, fantastic worlds. Most of them were written down by scholars some time between the eighth and the nineteenth centuries. Such tales can stimulate our imaginations and begin to help us to 'enter the minds' of our ancestors.

Second, are stories that can be created, using historical or archaeological evidence, to suggest the lives of the people and place. Such stories can simply illuminate day to day living or they can describe more dramatic occasions like a burial, a wedding, a harvest festival, a pilgrimage or a battle. Where historical records are available they can, of course, also tell a 'true story' of what actually happened.

A good story told well has an immediacy which captures the attention, touches the heart and stimulates the imagination. It can also deepen the sense of identity people feel with their ancestors and help them to

ENGLISH HERITAGE

Hugh Lupton at Portchester Castle, Hampshire.

understand who they are today. It can even inspire. In other words, stories reach the parts logical lectures and analytical explanations seldom reach! Stories touch the whole person. They are also easily remembered and enjoyable to tell, to hear and to retell.

Children respond naturally to stories with enthusiasm and interest. Though stories should primarily be told for their own sake, they can link with, or be a starting point for, other work across the curriculum.

This book aims to show:

■ why stories and storytelling are so important

■ how the oral tradition ('the Tree of Tales') has developed and grown in Britain over the millenia

■ what kind of stories are appropriate to tell at which kind of historic site

■ how to learn to tell, rather than read, stories

■ what preparation to do before a storytelling visit

■ how an appreciation of stories and an understanding of history can be furthered after such a visit

The book is aimed primarily at teachers, particularly those working with children in the 7 to 14 age range.

However it will also be of value to anyone who is interested in knowing more about how the rich story heritage of these islands can be linked to places of special historic importance.

One word of warning
We can never know with certainty what stories were told, especially at prehistoric sites. Stories left no 'hard evidence' until they were written down. So in what follows we are only suggesting the kind of stories that might have been told, based on written records, on the surviving oral tradition and on extant comparable cultures in other parts of the world. Inevitably this means making the occasional imaginative leap!

This leads to a second word of warning. This book is not written in the impartial language of an archaeologist or historian. Though there are in places, rational explanations, more often than not we are in the world of the storyteller. So, be prepared to 'suspend disbelief'!

HISTORY OF STORYTELLING

It is said that when a certain wise man saw trouble threatening his people he went into the forest, lit a fire and said a special prayer. Thus misfortune was averted. Before the wise man died he passed on some of his knowledge to another. So when trouble came to the land again the second wise man went to the same place in the forest and called out: 'Oh God, I do not know how to light a fire but I can still say the prayer.' Again trouble was averted. Still later another wise man went into the forest at a time of crisis and said: 'Lord, I cannot light the fire nor do I know the prayer, but at least I know the place. Let that be enough.' And it was enough. The danger passed. Then it fell to a fourth wise man to overcome misfortune. From his armchair he spoke to God. 'I cannot light a fire nor do I remember the prayer. I cannot even find the place in the forest. All I can do is tell the story. May this be enough.' And it was. For God made people because he likes stories.

BEGINNINGS

In the beginning was the word. Not the written word but the spoken word, formed by lips and tongue, carried on the breath, given voice over vocal chords, sounded once, heard once and then gone, vanished into the air.

In the beginning was language. Sounds that meant something. Names of animals, people, places and spirits; descriptions of colour, size, shape and feel; actions of going and coming, sleeping and waking, cooking and eating; explanations of how to find yams, honey and fish; tales of when the great mammoth was killed, of why the moon is born, grows full and dies.

In the beginning was the story. Stories were told: of how the world came to be the way it is; of the sun, the moon and the stars; of animals and birds, half human, half beast, magical, powerful and wise; of trees with roots going deep and branches spreading wide; of the first man and woman; of love, death and the hunt; of heroic adventures; of monsters and giants; of another world peopled by spirits, demons and gods.

Such was the stuff of story, told over and over again around campfires and beside hearths late into the night, night after night, all winter long. Fending off fears and the cold, firing imaginations, creating laughter and understanding, the stories brought magic and grandeur to a humdrum, everyday world. They explained to people the nature of the universe. And they showed them how to live.

ENGLISH HERITAGE

Shaman dancing.

STORYTELLERS

Stories came from the minds and mouths of living storytellers, the ones

ENGLISH HERITAGE

charged with passing on tradition. Their knowledge contained everything: from basic survival information to cautionary tales, from inspirational examples to accounts of the sacred foundations of life. They were historians, philosophers, teachers, preachers, poets, magicians and comics; their words justified the values of their society. Through their stories individuals were located within the circles of family, community, nature and the universe; were given a sense of what was expected of them in life, of what might come to them after death. So it was that tellers of tales helped to create meaning, safety and purpose for all from the beginning of human time.

At first the storytellers were shamans, medicine men and women, with magical powers and a deep knowledge of the sacred stories, the myths, of their people. These stories, often told in long song-chant cycles, contained the core values and beliefs of the tribe and were at the same time crucial aids to survival. Not surprisingly they were the greatest treasure that anyone could possess. Shamans were not judged by the things they owned but by the stories they knew, the rituals they were authorised to conduct, the dances they could perform.

Later storytellers became professional bards and were taken into the employ of chieftains and princes, queens and emperors. In the royal

ENGLISH HERITAGE

Brian Pearson with a group of special needs children at Wall Roman Site, Staffordshire.

courts they proclaimed genealogies and entertained the nobility by graphically depicting the exploits of favoured knights and warriors. In 'Beowulf' the king's poet is described as 'a man laden with eloquence, his mind charged with story, who remembered so many things of old.' The tales told by these bards may have begun as poetic accounts of real events, but after generations of embellishment they became the great heroic legends.

With the coming of literacy there was a decline in the aristocratic demand for bearers of an oral tradition. Their role was taken over by poets, players and romantic novelists. However among the ordinary people, still illiterate, storytellers continued to have an important educating and entertaining role to play. So, around cottage hearths all over Britain, tellers of folktales plied their art, from time immemorial through to the Industrial Revolution.

The heroes and heroines of their stories were often nameless beggars, fisherfolk, millers or woodcutters, who, with the aid of wise women, talking animals, magical objects or honest intent, often ended up being blessed with good fortune. Their daughters and sons sometimes even married royalty. These stories contained the vernacular wisdom of the people.

At the beginning of the nineteenth century the disruptions caused by new industrial patterns of life and work began to undermine the role of the living storyteller. Mass literacy and later the media seemed destined to drive this increasingly rare creature into extinction. In mid-twentieth century Britain the living storyteller who was still part of an unbroken oral tradition survived only among the travellers and in the remote rural areas of Scotland and Ireland.

SOME DEFINITIONS

Myth Myths are about animals of power, spirit ancestors, gods or goddesses and their sacred or supernatural actions in creating sky and earth, life and death, seasons and elements, themselves, people and the laws people must obey to survive. Myths are the oldest stories.

Legend Legends may start with a grain of historical truth, but they grow into fantastic tales. They are about the exploits and adventures of named heroes and heroines who are usually of royal stock but born in unusual circumstances. These characters have superhuman powers as rulers, warriors, bards or magicians. Though their lives may be cut short their story lives on.

Folktale Folktales (or wondertales) are about ordinary people living in an extraordinary, magical world of giants and witches, dragons and dwarfs, talking animals, enchanted forests, kings and queens, castles and cottages, good fortune for the humble, decline and fall for the haughty.

In addition there are also fairy stories, animal fables, sagas and romances which often draw heavily on the oral tradition but which have, to a greater or lesser extent, been consciously created by literary authors.

History History is an account, usually written, of what happened in the past. It is often, almost by necessity, presented in a narrative form. Though based on fact an historical story will vary according to the viewpoint of the witness or interpreter. In time historical events may be distorted and embellished and assume the character of legendary history.

These definitions are only general guides and should not be taken as rigid categories. Many stories include elements from more than one category.

WHY TELL STORIES . . . ?

STORY AND THE NATIONAL CURRICULUM: ENGLISH

The first aim of National Curriculum English is to develop knowledge, skills and understanding in speaking and listening; in other words, in oracy. From the beginning emphasis is put on the importance of listening attentively to stories, of responding to them and retelling them. It is stated, for example, that pupils should be able to:

■ 'recount events and narrate stories'; 'talk about the characters; say what they like or dislike about a story...'; 'compose a story with others'.

■ 'relate real or imaginary events in a connected narrative which conveys meaning to a group, for example, tell a story with a beginning, middle and end...'

■ 'participate in a presentation; for example, improvise a scene from a story or poem...'

■ 'use, and understand the use of, role play in teaching and learning; for example, to explore an aspect of history...'

There is, then, ample support from the National Curriculum for developing the practice of storytelling. However there are other sound educational reasons for developing such a practice.

Story and Thinking Scholars assert that there are two principal modes of thought, two distinctive ways of making sense of our worlds. One is the narrative mode. The other is the logical or scientific mode. The two, though complementary, are not reducible to one another. Narrative is the way we make our experience meaningful by telling stories about it. It is the older, primary way of thinking, something humans have probably done ever since learning to speak.

For millenia people passed down their knowledge and wisdom by word of mouth. This required feats of memory uncommon in the modern world. Such feats were made possible by using stories. It is as if stories were designed to be easily remembered. For, in a story, one thing invariably leads to the next; the themes are familiar, the characters larger than life, the situations recognisable. Stories are often funny, frightening, tragic or heart-warming; they make use of repetitions and rhymes, sayings and songs: all of which helps them to lodge readily in the mind. Modern experiments have shown that people asked to remember abstract formulae or lists of meaningless words will often make up a story to assist their memory.

Writing made possible a far greater degree of abstraction and analysis. It led, ultimately, to a rapid development of the logical way of thinking which, in turn, brought extraordinary changes to the world. Indeed, the logical mind seemed to supercede the narrative mind entirely.

However, the storytelling brain is still there, at work in everyday conversations, fascinated by yarns and tales of every kind, capable of comprehending and remembering as much now as ever. It is a faculty that could be much more widely used in educational practice today.

Story and Feeling In traditional stories the full range of human emotions are expressed and therefore evoked in an audience. So children listening to such stories will encounter many situations and emotional responses that they have not experienced personally. Through the story they may come to feel loss, grief, fear, anger, jealousy, stupidity, greed and arrogance; and they may also come to feel or appreciate hope, beauty, courage, wisdom, humility, perseverance, love, wit, strength, gentleness and compassion. They will thus be helped to come to terms with difficult emotions and, at the same time, to develop positive qualities and values.

Story and Imagination Listening to stories stimulates the capacity to see pictures in the mind's eye and nourishes the imagination. For example, when we try to visualise a sky-god or Mother Earth, the wind eagle or a talking horse, stone giants or the black witch, a cranky king or a warrior queen; when we hear of their schemes, their quests, their journeys to the underworld; when we learn about the world tree or the cauldron of inspiration: then we are given themes, metaphors, characters and potentialities to enrich our imaginations and dreams. The stories deepen and broaden the mind with which we create and help us to see our own lives, our own stories, with a touch of grandeur and imagination.

ENGLISH HERITAGE

Restormel Castle, Cornwall.

Story and Expression Hearing or telling a story is very different from reading or being read to. It engrosses us in quite another way. Listening we are all eyes and ears, taking in every nuance of voice, expression and gesture as the tale spills out from within the storyteller. In telling we take command of all our faculties and cast a net over our audience, drawing them in with a magical spell created from the subtlety and range of the voice, the movements of hand and eye, the power of the living word and, above all, the strange enchantment of the story.

In breathing life into stories and making them our own, we first need to know how to begin so that we catch our audience. Then we have to feel ourselves into the characters and find a way of expressing each one distinctly. We need to be able to describe action with vitality and paint pictures with words: and, if possible, to use humour. We need to develop a sense of rhythm and timing so that we can build to a climax and end when the listener feels complete. And always we must be the narrator, the one who was there when it happened and who is here now, carrying the tale across generations, bringing it alive once again for today's people, today's heroes and heroines.

In short, a diverse array of expressive skills are required. So becoming a storyteller promotes, at the very least, a refinement of the ability to use facial expressions, gestures and tone of voice to communicate meaning. It helps children and teachers to develop their expressive powers to the full.

ENGLISH HERITAGE

Brian Pearson at Wall Roman Site, Staffordshire.

Story and Cultural Identity

Many have claimed that it is through our stories that we know who we are. Laurens van der Post, for example, speaking about a Bushman friend, says:

'The supreme expression of his spirit was in his stories. He was a wonderful storyteller. The story was his most sacred possession. These people knew what we do not: that without a story you have not got a nation, a culture or a civilisation. Without a story of your own to live you haven't got a life of your own.'
(In 'Patterns of Renewal', 1962, P.9).

Today many of our stories come from books, literary creations of the last few hundred years. But there is a deeper level of story, the stories that have been told over and over again, by word of mouth, since time immemorial. Stories of the Oral Tradition. Within these stories can be found the universal truths and wild imaginations of the pre-literate peoples who inhabited these islands over the last few millenia. By hearing and retelling them we step out of our own time and touch our roots, an important source of cultural identity.

Story and Enjoyment Last but not least, good storytelling is, to the teller and listener alike, pure pleasure. To put it simply, it's fun!

Avebury, Wiltshire.

ENGLISH HERITAGE

STORY AND THE NATIONAL CURRICULUM: HISTORY

National Curriculum History recognises sites as valuable historical sources and suggests, for example, that pupils should be able to 'talk about how information gained from a historic site can be used to reconstruct the way of life of its former inhabitants'. The inference is that the information will be observed and deduced by examining the physical remains at a site. However, insight into the lives of former inhabitants can also come from hearing stories about the place, and stories that were once told there. In this way children's 'historical imagination' may be awakened. The telling of such stories is also a way of keeping the spirit of the place and its people alive! National Curriculum History stresses from the beginning the importance of learning through stories from different periods and cultures, including myths and legends of Britain, stories about historic events and fictional stories set in the past. It underlines the continuing relevance of the story by stating, for example, that pupils should be able to:

■ 'place in sequence events in a story about the past'; 'understand that stories may be about real people or fictional characters'; 'show an awareness that stories about the past can give different versions of what happened'.

It is also suggested that stories may help pupils to:

■ 'suggest reasons why people in the past acted as they did. Identify differences between the past and the present'; 'identify differences between times in the past'; 'recognise that over time some things changed and others stayed the same'.

Storytelling at historic sites is especially appropriate for study units which cover:

■ early peoples, from stone age hunter gatherers and first farmers to the Iron Age Celts and Romans

■ invasions of the Saxons, Vikings and Normans

■ events of the medieval period.

ENGLISH HERITAGE

Rievaulx Abbey, North Yorkshire.

During all this time stories from the Oral Tradition were a primary means of communication. The National Curriculum suggests that these societies should, where possible, be explored through local examples. It is therefore appropriate to visit and tell stories at sites ranging from once inhabited caves to burial chambers, stone circles, hillforts, abandoned villages, Roman forts and villas, holy wells, priories, abbeys, churches, castles, mansions and merchant houses.

Storytelling can also be used effectively in more thematic study units such as those on reading and writing, food and farming, domestic life, exploration and frontiers. In these themes it would be legitimate to draw on stories from other cultures of the world.

Story as an Historical Source

Traditional stories can rarely be dated precisely, but nevertheless certain kinds of stories can, when analysed, tell us much about the societies which created them. Celtic legends, for example, evoke the daily lives, the beliefs and the values of Iron Age Britain, especially the warrior aristocracy. Arthurian romances tell us mostly about courtly life in the Middle Ages, though there are echoes back to the sixth century historic Arthur

and forward to nineteenth century poets. The majority of folktales are suggestive more of the ordinary people whose lives changed comparatively little from the end of Roman rule through to the Industrial Revolution.

So, as well as their value as stories for their own sake, legends and folktales can be very useful as historical sources.

Historical Stories
Sometimes there is a fine line between the legends that exist about a place and the stories of what 'really' happened. When the history of a site is known it is important to find a way of telling that story effectively. Unfortunately guide books often offer rather dry accounts which may need to be imaginatively penetrated if the site's story is to come alive. Sometimes this process can be aided by reading historical novelists who specialise in bringing the past to life. An historical story based on the known facts and told well will have a compelling effect on listeners, even though it may not have the form of a traditional tale.

Perhaps all stories told at an historic site should be presented as being true, with the understanding that 'truth and lies live in the same house, and they both come out of the same door.' That way children can sort out the difference for themselves and playfully.

THE TREE OF TALES

This section aims to suggest the kind of stories that are appropriate to tell at a wide range of historic sites in Britain. To bring a site alive it seems most fitting to tell, as far as possible, the stories that might have been told by the people who lived there when the place was inhabited. These are stories from the oral tradition, 'The Tree of Tales', and can tell us much about the lives, beliefs and imaginations of the people who made each place their home. For each period a visit to a particular type of site is suggested, and for each type of site examples are given of the kind of story that was probably told then and could be told now.

Stories often seem to reflect peoples' religious beliefs, and so they change as those beliefs change. In each age something is gained, something is lost. The oldest stories, like the pre-Christian creation myths, are now almost completely forgotten. Later stories introduce new dimensions, whilst including distorted fragments of earlier tales. Familiar themes find different, sometimes more fully elaborated expressions. Tales that are found in other parts of the world turn up in an English, Irish, Scottish or Welsh variation. Gradually the great 'Tree of Tales' grows. One can imagine the trunk as the old myths of nature and creation; the limbs and branches as the heroic legends; and the twigs and leaves as the folktales - all drawing sap from the same fertile story ground. And now we have the privilege of being able to choose stories from almost any part of that great Tree.

ENGLISH HERITAGE

THE HUNTER GATHERERS

The first people to live in the lands of Britain (while it was still connected to the European mainland) survived by hunting and gathering. There weren't many of them. They moved freely from place to place following the ripening of the fruits and the movement of the herds. They didn't try to change the Earth. They lived closely with it. They made simple tools and used fire to cook and keep warm. They shared food within their clan and reverently disposed of their dead. Though we have no direct evidence we suppose - from art of the period and from comparable cultures elsewhere who survived into modern times - that they told stories. This was the way humankind lived for 99% of its two million year long evolution, until the beginning of farming just a few thousand years ago.

There are not many hunter-gatherer sites in Britain and it would be tempting to skip the whole period were it not for the fact that it played such a major part in the development of so many important human ideas and skills. Also, stories that probably originated then have been told, in various forms, ever since.

Animal Stories We can get an idea of the stories that might have been told by the first people in Britain by looking at the myths of the hunter-gatherer peoples who have survived into modern times in Africa, Australia and the Americas. They live as part of nature. As a result of their close observation of prey and predators they are intimate with the character of the wild animals who share their world. They dream about them and even imagine themselves to be such animals. In their art they paint animals with great sensitivity, as did some of our hunter-gatherer forebears. In their dances they become the animals of the hunt, sometimes wearing their skins and horns, imitating their movements with empathy, skill and humour.

It is not surprising that the stories of hunter-gatherers are often about how animals made the world and taught humans their most important lessons. The animals in these stories are extra-ordinary. They have enormous creative power and whilst animal in form they think, talk and act like humans. This suggests a close identity between people and animals, as if animals have human minds and humans have the capacity to take on animal minds.

In the creation mythology of hunter-gatherer peoples many animals have helped in the great task of making the world - raven, eagle, swan, bear, wolf, boar, stag, salmon, frog and ant, to name but a few. For example, the Kwakiutl people of the Pacific north-west tell the story of how Raven brought daylight to the world; the Inuit tell of Eagle giving people the gift of song and dance; the northern Australians have a story of the Rainbow Bird taking fire from Crocodile and putting it into the heart of every tree so people could use it. Such stories often also explain how animals come to have the characteristics they have today.

It seems likely that the religious impulse of early peoples was towards animals, both as an expression of wonder and as a desire to experience communion with them. This is sometimes called 'totemism' and suggests the origin of animal stories, still popular to this day in fables, fairy tales and children's books.

Mother Earth Not only were the first people close to animals. They were close to the elements too: to the strength of the wind and the feel of the rain; to the movement of the sun, the phases of the moon and the patterns made by stars in the night sky; to change, always change; to death and new life. They felt the body of the Earth like a human body, a body with arms and legs, head and hair, eyes and teeth, lungs and breasts, heart and blood and navel. They felt it like a nurturing body, sometimes a harsh and cruel body, but mostly a body that gave food and drink, rest and play; a body that gave new life. The body of a mother. Mother Earth.

So some of the first creation stories were about the elements, about why the wind blows, why there is day and night, about the shape and colours of the rainbow. There were also stories about the land, how it was shaped into hills, rocks, rivers and lakes by the power of creative ancestors. These beings, animal/human spirits, emerged from beneath the ground at time's beginning and made epic journeys across the landscape, leaving a trail of sacred places and stories to be told - the songlines or dreaming tracks of the Aboriginal Australians.

Hunter-gatherers were also probably the first to tell stories about the Earth Mother, the Goddess, the creator and sustainer of all life. These stories would have been told in rituals designed to enhance the fertility of people and the animals and plants on which their lives depended. Fertility was a theme that was to continue for many millenia to come.

Sites for Stories There are few hunter-gatherer sites in Britain. The most evocative are the sites of once inhabited caves, such Kent's Cavern in Devon, King Arthur's Cave in the Forest of Dean, Pontnewydd Cave in Clwyd and Church Hole Cave in Derbyshire. But the early hunter gatherers also lived in open sites by lakes and rivers and, later, in forest clearings. Any of these places would be suitable for telling the oldest stories, stories of creation, of the animals, of Mother Earth.

ENGLISH HERITAGE

Raven breaking open the bag of daylight.

THE FIRST FARMERS (c.5000 – c.2000 BC)

About 8000 years ago the sea level rose dramatically, cutting the British Isles off from continental Europe and shaping the coastline we know today. About a thousand years later people began to cultivate the land, for the first time actively working alongside nature to produce a surplus of food. For the early farmers these changes were far reaching. People had to think a year ahead, preparing, planting and harvesting the crop in accordance with the annual seasonal cycle. They no longer needed to be nomads, but could settle down and build more permanent dwellings and settlements. They were able to produce a surplus of food which could be translated into material wealth. So farming meant not only the hard work of tending crops but also finding ways to protect their land and wealth. It also brought the domestication of animals -

cows, goats, sheep, horses, pigs and fowl. This new mastery over animals may have led to a loss of the old religious veneration for them and the beginning of a belief that beasts had been made for humans; and the stories probably reflected this change.

The Gods and Goddesses

It may be that for the earliest peoples creative power was invested in animals. These beings - animal in form, human in thought and godlike in power - were the creators of the world as well as the source of life and wisdom. They were, therefore, the focus of worship and the subject of many stories. Although there is no clear evidence about the religious and story life of early British farmers, by looking at the changes which took place when agriculture was developed elsewhere, we see indications that the focus of creative power shifted from the animals to the gods. In these cultures it

is the gods and goddesses, rather than animal beings, who were thought to have created the world and given the gifts of knowledge to people.

The gods were more human in form but had supernatural power over natural elements like wind, sea, sun, thunder, rain and earth. For example, in ancient Sumer, where some of the earliest farming took place, Anu, the sky god, was the source of law and order. This law was enforced by Enlil, the wind god, who executed the will of Anu and guaranteed order against chaos. A third great power was the earth, Nintu, 'the lady who gives birth', the inexhaustible and mysterious source of all life. Fertilising the womb of Nintu with life giving waters was the male water god, Enki, also the god of wisdom and creative thought. In and behind everything important people sensed the presence of gods. There was, for example, a reed goddess who produced

Knowlton Earthworks, Dorset.

ENGLISH HERITAGE

reeds, used for building houses, taught the shepherd the tunes he played on his reed pipe and inspired the scribe who wrote with a reed pen.

There were also gods associated with animals, but now more often domesticated species such as the sow, the bull, the ram and the horse. One early British goddess was Brigit, goddess of fire and inspiration, who was associated with cattle. Another was Cerridwen, the White Sow goddess. There is a Celtic story about her bringing to Wales the gifts of wheat, barley, bees and her own young. This seems to be about the beginnings of farming and suggests that the story may actually have an early origin.

A Greek story about the naming of Athens reflects the same preoccupation of the first farming communities. It tells of how Poseidon, god of the sea, competed with Athene, goddess of wisdom, to give the greatest gift to humanity. Poseidon gave the horse, a powerful creature of great value but destined to carry men into battle; Athene gave the olive tree, providing food and soothing oil, shade, timber and fuel. This was judged the greater gift and, so the story goes, the city of Athens was named after her.

Gods and goddesses were thought to control human destiny. They could appear in everyday life in a variety of guises, even as other people, and had to be appeased through the rituals of prayer and sacrifice. For example bulls were sometimes killed and their blood spilled on the fields to promote the regrowth of vegetation.

The Seasons: Death and Fertility

Life and death are perhaps the eternal human preoccupations, but with the coming of farming this concern gained a new perspective. It is possible, for example, that people became more aware of the seasons and how the annual cycle mirrors the life cycle of birth, growth, maturity, death and, so they believed, rebirth. Rituals may have been held to mark the solstices. In some farming cultures it was noticed that the death of winter is always followed by the birth of new life, so sacrifices were made to encourage fertility and rebirth.

The moon, which appears to die and be reborn every month, was taken on as an important natural symbol. So too was the snake. Its ability to shed its skin and so renew its youth earned it a

White Sow goddess who was thought to have brought the gifts of grain, bees and piglets to the first farmers of Britain.

ENGLISH HERITAGE

reputation as a master of rebirth. But perhaps the prime symbol of fertility was the Earth Goddess. She was a figure of great importance in many farming cultures. She was often thought of as triple in nature: the youthful maiden, the pregnant mother and the dying crone reflecting the phases of the moon, the seasons of the year and the cycle of life. Though recent archaeological evidence suggests that this time in Britain may not have been as peaceful as some have thought, it is nonetheless possible that there was less conflict then than in later periods. It may also be that society at this time was less patriarchal, with women having a more prominent role than subsequently.

Sites for Stories

For 2000 years after the introduction of farming to Britain, it would seem, from the evidence of surviving burial chambers, that there was a strong association with death, rebirth and the worship of ancestors. Some of the stone tombs, quoits and barrows built during that time have lasted to this day. What happened in them we can only guess, as there is no oral tradition or written record to link us with them. However it is possible they were sites of ritual where

the dead were honoured, where songs and stories were chanted, where new life was welcomed. Today they are still suitable places to tell stories of ancestors, of the Otherworld, about fertility and the renewal of life.

Later many of the old tombs were blocked up and henges and stone circles, like those at Avebury and Stonehenge, were built. These structures - circular ditches with embankments, sometimes enclosing rings of stones - do not seem to have been defensive and were perhaps ceremonial in purpose. Periodically they were probably the focal point for large numbers of people. Whilst it is possible that a creation mythology was still being enacted to explain the cosmos, it may be that wedding rites, the harvest and the return of the sun after midwinter were some of the main causes for celebration and ritual at these stone circles.

Although we have no way of knowing what tales were told at this time, stories carefully chosen (and perhaps adapted) from comparable farming cultures in other parts of the world can work well to bring these extraordinary places alive. Circle dances are also appropriate to perform.

METALS: THE AGES OF BRONZE AND IRON

The discovery of how to smelt and shape metals into hard, sharp and often beautiful tools, weapons and ornaments eventually affected society and culture at every level. With bronze, an alloy of copper and tin, it was possible to beat out shields and make slashing swords, thus increasing the deadliness of battle.

The manufacture of high quality goods of bronze and gold, led to the improvement of trading networks and more work for the itinerant merchant, an agent, as always, of cultural cross fertilisation. Farming developments, like the ox drawn plough, enabled the production of more food and therefore the support of a larger population. Some land became worn out. Pressure on land began to increase.

Around 500 BC a new metal took over: iron. It was more common than bronze, so weapons and artefacts of iron became more widely available. Perhaps this, together with the growing pressure on the land, led to a further militarisation of society. In the few centuries before the arrival of the Romans, numerous hillforts were built all over Britain. These redoubts seem to have been defended settlements, though they also may have been statements of prestige as well as grain stores and refuges for cattle and people in times of conflict. Some scholars suggest that they indicate a tribalised society ruled by chiefs and a warrior nobility, where metalsmiths took pride of place amongst craftsmen and where religious life was directed by Druids. This view receives some support from the Celtic

legends that have survived from that period.

We can assume that Celtic religion was built on earlier foundations, with the cycle of the year and the seasonal festivals still, as with any farming society, occupying an important role. Sacred places for the Druids were woodland groves of oak where the mistletoe was regarded as a plant of special power. Druids were also the judges in Celtic society, and sacrifice possibly played a part in keeping law and order.

Celtic chiefs were sufficiently wealthy to be able to patronise both artists and poets. The work produced by artists reflects the taste of warriors who

Ancient Technology Centre, Cranborne, Dorset.

ENGLISH HERITAGE

enjoyed the luxury and personal magnificence of fine brooches, bracelets, mirrors, necklaces, helmets and scabbards. And the poets? They were the bards, storytellers who recounted great legends about the Age of Heroes.

The Age of Heroes

In the Heroic Age many of the creative powers formerly attributed to animals or gods appeared to shift to the heroes. Although animals and nature still had a place in the heroic world they were essentially residual. And gone was the supremacy of the Goddess. She retreated to the dark and hidden places, and though in Ireland she retained a formidable presence, on the face of it she was superceded by the hero. For this was the age of the patriarch, the warrior, the age of victory and defeat. Skill in battle was the greatest arbiter of success. The hero assumed the mantle of the gods and undertook dangerous journeys and stupendous feats, overcoming evil monsters and overwhelming odds. Unlike the gods, however, heroes proved to be mortal. But though their lives may have been cut short, the valour of their deeds lived on in legend.

The Heroic Age also coincided with the beginnings of writing. As a result many of the great legends were written down, two of the most famous in Europe being Homer's 'Iliad' and 'Odyssey'. Some reference to Celtic legends is made in the writings of Roman observers like Julius Caesar and Tacitus. But the Celtic tradition was not directly written down till between the 6th and 11th century AD. The authors were often clerics who sometimes imposed a Christian filter on their work. They were also by then transcribing an oral tradition which was both fragmentary and overlaid with subsequent invention and history. However, for the Celtic period, stretching from c.500 BC to c. AD 500, we can for the first time draw our stories from written sources.

Legends from Ireland

The oldest and most extensive material comes from Ireland. 'The Book of Invasions' recounts the waves of invaders who colonised Ireland, beginning with the descendents of Noah and culminating in the arrival of the Tuatha De Danann, the peoples of the goddess Dana, who themselves were eventually overcome by the Celts. The Tuatha, it is said, withdrew to the wild

Cu Culann, the Celtic hero, in battle frenzy.

places of Ireland, the fairy hills, where they still dwell today. The second cycle of stories, the 'Ulster Cycle', is about the warriors of King Conchobar of Ulster, especially the greatest hero of them all, Cu Culann. These stories are based on events thought to have taken place around 100 BC and AD 100, the heart of

the Celtic period. They are Celtic legends par excellance. A third cycle of stories, the Fenian Cycle, are about Fionn Mac Cumhaill (pronounced Finn MacCool) and the Fiana, and are dated to the 3rd century AD. Fionn was a hunter rather than a warrior and the tales of the Fiana are more lyrical and romantic than heroic. There is also a Historical Cycle of stories which centre on various high-kings of Ireland whose dates range from the third century BC to AD 800.

Legends from Wales

The legends preserved in 'The Mabinogion' are set in Wales and originated in the pre-Christian Celtic era. They have survived only in a fragmentary form, but it is possible that originally they were about the birth, life and death of Pryderi, as he is the only character who appears in all Four Branches of the Mabinogion. However in two of the Branches he is now only a peripheral figure. The First Branch is about Pwyll, his sojourn in the Otherworld, his marriage to Rhiannon (the horse goddess) and the bizarre birth and upbringing of their son Pryderi. The Second Branch concerns the marriage of

Branwen, sister of Bran the Blessed and Efnisien the trouble maker, to the king of Ireland. Bran leads an expedition to Ireland to rescue Branwen from the problems she has due to Efnisien's ill deeds. Pryderi is among the seven survivors of the ensuing battle who return to Wales. In the Third Branch Pryderi and his companions fall under an enchantment and wander around a desolate land until the spell is broken. The Fourth Branch describes Pryderi's death, but the stories centre upon the magician Gwydion and his role in the birth, upbringing and marriage to Blodeuedd (woman of flowers) of Lleu Llaw Gyffes, the Fair One of the Deft Hand. Other stores in 'The Mabinogion' include ones about Lud, who saved Britain from three terrible plagues and whose name may be referred to in London ('Ludtown'); and Culhwch, whose epic quest for Olwen was assisted by Arthur in one of the earliest references to the legendary king.

'History of the Kings of Britain'

This is the title of a book written in the twelfth century by Geoffrey of Monmouth. He claimed it to be a true history of these islands back as far as the time of Troy. However, although some of his characters were real historical figures, his work was largely based on legends that had been orally transmitted, and his own literary invention. A good part of the book is devoted to the story of Merlin and Arthur, but the early chapters refer to the pre-Roman period and so contain legends pertaining to the Celts. In spite of Geoffrey's own embellishments his book remains a good source of stories set in the thousand years from about 500 BC to AD 500.

Sites for Stories

There are hundreds of hillfort sites in Britain which could have been homes to the heroes. Some, like Maiden Castle, are truly monumental in scale; others, like Oswestry, are well formed but more modest; some are barely visible at all. However all are a vivid reminder of Celtic times when it was often safer to gather on a defended hilltop, though probably most of the time people lived in the valleys. Nowadays they can be exposed and blustery places, but on calm days or in sheltered spots they are the ideal settings for Celtic legends. Hut circles are a homelier reminder of pre-Roman days and also appropriate places for the telling of Celtic tales. In some areas of the country are the remains of entire Celtic villages, for example, at Chysauster in Cornwall. Here it is possible to imagine a farming and tin-panning life into which storytelling fitted in an integral way.

Finally it is reasonable to assume that Celtic legends written down in the early Medieval period may have been told by bards in the courts and castles of the Middle Ages.

'In an old Welsh story about the birth of Taliesin, Gwion Bach is chased by Ceridwen for swallowing three drops of inspiration which she has carefully brewed for a year and a day and which were intended for her own dim-witted son. Gwion Bach, now in possession of magical powers, first turns himself into a hare, but Ceridwen becomes a hound and follows him the closer; Gwion then becomes a fish but she becomes an otter and followes him the closer; he becomes a dove but she becomes a hawk and follows him the closer; finally he becomes a grain of wheat but she becomes a hen and swallows Gwion Bach up. After nine months she gives birth to a beautiful baby boy who goes on to become the great poet Taliesin.'

THE ROMANO-BRITISH PERIOD

The Roman conquest of Britain roughly marks the beginning of recorded history, and so the changes of that period are well known. The Romans were efficient and well organised. Their superior discipline and centralised control enabled them to overcome the unruly vigour of the Celtic tribes, where each man or woman fought as individuals rather than in any unified battle formation. Within twenty years of the elephant-graced visit of Emperor Claudius, the population of the lowlands had been subdued and the power of the Druids was destroyed. The Romans then began constructing a road network radiating out from London and building the first real towns of these islands, with villas, temples and baths. They also offered new gods in exchange for the old.

The First History

Several Roman observers, starting with Caesar himself, wrote about Britain and recounted their own, inevitably biased, view of the stages of the conquest. Using these sources, together with archaeological evidence it is possible to build up stories about actual events, for example: the sacking of Maiden Castle by the Roman legions; Caradog's last stand on Llanymynech Hill, his escape and subsequent betrayal by the Brigantian queen, Cartimandua, his dignified speech to his captors in Rome; the slaughter of the Druids and other refugees on their island stronghold of Mon; the uprising led by Boudica, at first wildy successful, in the end utterly crushed.

To these historical events can be added legends which, though containing a kernel of truth, have been embellished through the ages to gloss over the Roman victory and place the native Britons in a better light. For example, Geoffrey of Monmouth tells of the encounter between Cassivellaunos and Caesar where the British high king emerges with dignity and valour, having seen off the Roman threat. And in 'The Mabinogion' there is the story about the Dream of Macsen, which describes how the Emperor Maximus came to Wales in search of the woman of his dreams.

The Gods Link Up

With the Romans came their pantheon of gods, some of whom - Mars, Mercury, Apollo,

ABOVE: **Caradog rallying his people before the Roman onslaught.**

RIGHT: **Maiden Castle, Dorset.**

ENGLISH HERITAGE

Jupiter and Minerva - were blended with the native gods of the Celts. For example Sulis, the Celtic sun goddess responsible for warming the waters at healing springs (such as those at Bath), was combined with Minerva to produce a Romano-Celtic deity of healing. Rosmerta, the Celtic goddess of plenty and good fortune, depicted pouring wine into a wooden tub, was paired with Mercury, the Roman god of commercial success and often seen with a heavy purse. Taranis, the Celtic sky-god, was equated with Jupiter. Both commanded thunder and lightning and, because of the association with hammering and the fire of the forge, were also regarded as gods of the smithy.

The Romans also had their own classical literature and were familiar with the mythology and oral traditions of Greece. Although it was many centuries before these classics made a major impact on British culture, it is reasonable to suppose that the stories of Greece and Rome had at least some currency in the camps and towns that spread around England and Wales during the 400 years of Roman occupation. It would be fitting, therefore, to retell such stories in the ruins of these historic sites today.

Sites for Stories

The native Britons viewed the approaching Roman army from their hilltop forts, so these are the places in which quasi-historical stories can be told about the resistance

ENGLISH HERITAGE

to, and the eventual triumph of, the Roman legions. Tacitus tells us, for example, that prior to the battle at Llanymynech Hill Caradog (or Caractacus) rushed around stirring up his troops and '*invoking that very day and that very battle as either the rebirth of liberty or the beginning of eternal servitude. He called upon his ancestors by name, those who had driven out Julius Caesar, the dictator. The valour of these men had preserved their descendants from the power of Roman officials and the imposition of tribute.*' One can imagine that the story of 'Cassivellaunos and Caesar', as retold by Geoffrey of Monmouth, would have been on the storyteller's lips the night before battle, especially as Cassivellaunos was Caradog's great grandfather. It's a story that may have been repeated at many hillforts, including Maiden Castle, where archaeologists have found evidence of a Roman siege and assault.

In the more peaceful years that followed the establishment of Roman rule, mines were dug and villas, baths, temples, roads and walled cities were built around England and in parts of Wales. Unfortunately many of the ruins at these sites are scarcely more than foundations today, as the stones were reused by later builders. Nevertheless there are some well known and well preserved sites - the baths at Bath, the town at St Albans, the villas at Lullingstone and Fishborne, the Saxon shore-fort at Portchester, city walls of Chester and Hadrian's Wall - where tales drawn from history and Romano-Celtic mythology can be told.

CENTURIES OF INVASION AND RESISTANCE: c. AD 440 - AD 1066

At the end of the Roman period in Britain it is often said that the country sank into an unenlightened age of darkness. This is because the regular urban rule of the Romans faded and because life became dominated by 'barbarians', men of action and power who did not care to keep an accurate record of events. For several centuries waves of such land-hungry invaders came to pillage and settle on these shores. The Picts, the Anglo-Saxons, the Danes, the Jutes and the Vikings arrived from various quarters to the north and east, each bringing their own cultural flavour to mingle with that of the Romano-British natives.

A slightly gentler invasion came in the form of a new religion, Christianity. Although the so-called Dark Ages were not a time of rapid cultural and economic development, nevertheless this new religion led to many changes on the social and spiritual front. Indeed, some say it was the monks who held the western world together during that period. Certainly many new stories became current in Britain then, including parables of biblical origin and stories of the saints.

It was also during this period that the most enduring and well developed of British legends were originally set - the legends of Arthur. Though Arthurian romances did not gain their fullest expression until the Medieval period they derive from a probable historic figure of the sixth century and draw on an oral tradition which began soon after. So from the storytelling point of view there is much light to be found in 'dark age' Britain!

The Coming of the Saints

The early Christians came to these islands during Roman times; the first person to achieve sainthood was Alban who was martyred at Verulanium, later to become St Albans. His story is told by the Venerable Bede in the 'Ecclesiastical History of the English People', written in the early eighth century.

As the Romans abandoned England, Patrick, a Christian Briton who had been captured by Irish pirates, began the conversion of Ireland. The Irish church developed a special character, independent of Rome. Its clerics sought

The dialogue of Patrick and Ossian.

wild and remote places in which to cultivate their learning. In some ways Christianity was grafted on to the pre-existing druidic religion, with sacred springs becoming holy wells, pagan rites being transposed for Christian purposes,

festivals of the changing seasons being incorporated into the Christian calendar. Some of Patrick's miracles even had a Celtic flavour. Once his prayers conjured up a heavy mist and caused an earthquake to shake the fortress of the king of Tara. Later he escaped by being transformed, with his followers, into a herd of deer. In the Irish storytelling tradition there is an account of a dialogue between Patrick and Ossian, son of Fionn Mac Cumaill, after Ossian's return from the land of the Ever Young. It is a fascinating exchange in which the fervent Christian tries unsuccessfully to convert the lamenting old Celt, who remembers only the virtues of life with the Fianna - the hunt, strength and bravery in battle, generosity and high living. It could be said that this debate between the hero and the saint marks the point in British cultural history when the supernatural creative power moved from the heroic to the saintly.

Bridget of Kildare followed in Patrick's footsteps and many of the qualities of the Celtic goddess Bridget became associated with her: the brightness of fire, symbolising the

sustaining spirit; the whiteness of cow's milk and the snowdrop, both symbolising new life. St Bridget's day falls at the beginning of February on Imbolc, the old Celtic festival marking the first signs of spring. After Bridget came Columba who brought the Celtic Christian church from Ireland to Scotland and the rest of Britain, establishing monasteries in Iona and Lindisfarne.

In AD 596 Pope Gregory the Great sent a mission to Britain led by Augustine, who established a church at Canterbury. The success of this mission led to a conflict with the Celtic Christians who differed with Rome on a number of points, including the so-called pelagian heresy, which denied the existence of original sin and declared that a man could further the work of Grace through his own will. This was unacceptable to popes in Rome who felt that it undermined their central authority. The matter was resolved in favour of Rome at the Synod of Whitby in AD 664.

Sites for Stories Books about the lives and legends of saints (hagiography) are numerous, so there are many sources for stories of the early Christian church. The miracles of the saints are reminiscent of an era when magic was thought commonplace. They belong with the mysterious 'dark ages', better, perhaps, than to later periods. However there are many places where saints' stories can be told, ranging from holy wells (such as Holywell in Clwyd) and sixth century chapels through to medieval priorys, abbeys, churches and even castles: anywhere, in short, where Christian teachings have been promulgated. Chaucer's 'Canterbury Tales' affirm both the tradition of pilgrimage to sacred places and the art of telling tales, and are therefore also a valuable source for stories at medieval religious sites.

The Legends of Arthur

If there was an historical Arthur he was probably a Romano-British chieftain who successfully led his warband against the invading Saxons and, after a final battle at Badon Hill (around AD 500), maintained peace in Britain for more than twenty years. One source attributes Arthur's military success to him carrying a banner with a portrait of the Virgin Mary into battle. If true this would make him the first Christian hero-king of Britain. But the historical Arthur is not so important. It is the legends surrounding him that are much more interesting, representing as they probably do the greatest and most complete legendary story in the British cultural tradition.

The earliest legends about Arthur date from the ninth century, some 300 years after his death, and derive from the Welsh oral tradition. In the story of 'Culhwch and Olwen' Arthur is asked by Culhwch, his nephew, for help in attaining the hand of Olwen, the daughter of Ysbathaden, chief of the giants. Arthur agrees to help and handpicks certain warriors for the task. Each one has fantastic powers: Cai, for example, can hold his breath under water for nine days and keep anything dry with his body heat; Cynthilig can guide people through a land he has never visited; Gwalchmai always finds what he is looking for; Gurir

LEFT: **Cleeve Abbey, Somerset.**   RIGHT: **Gawain and the Loathly Lady.**

understands all languages. With the help of Arthur and his warriors Culhwch achieves all of Ysbathaden's seemingly impossible demands, culminating in hunting the Wildboar, and wins Olwen. It is an extraordinary tale, quite unlike the medieval romances of King Arthur and his knights that were to follow.

It was Geoffrey of Monmouth who, in the twelfth century, launched Arthur's career as a literary creation. By embroidering the oral tradition with his own fiction he set the Arthurian story more in his own time. He told of Merlin's prophecy about a struggle between a red and a white dragon, symbolising conflict between Britons and Saxons, and about the coming of Arthur to protect Britain. It was Merlin who then helped to bring about Arthur's strange conception and who

oversaw his early education. Much of Geoffrey's story concerned the battles fought by Arthur and his warriors to fend off invaders and then to conquer Europe, but he also wrote about Guinevere, Arthur's queen and Merdred, his newphew. However it fell to the French author Chretien de Troyes to introduce the idea of chivalry, where King Arthur reigned over a court of heroic knights who met at the Round table and who, with Lancelot supreme amongst them, travelled the world in search of love and adventure.

It was not until 1485 that Sir Thomas Malory wrote the definitive, 'Le Morte D'Arthur'. Malory drew on both French and British literary traditions, but broadened the picture by telling many

tales about Arthur's principal knights. His version has been modernised, adapted and developed by numerous authors ever since. In spite of the ideals of chivalry held by Arthur's knights - to be loyal to king, family and beloved; to be courteous and gentle, especially to women; to be courageous at all times; to show mercy to those who ask for it; to be a man of honour and therefore highly esteemed by others - the romance of Arthur ended in tragedy. With the collapse of the Round Table a legendary golden age came to a close.

Sites for Stories Most of the Arthurian legends we know are products of literary imaginations more than oral tradition. However, as they occupy such a dominant position in the legendary history of Britain, they are obvious stories to tell at historic sites.

The most natural places for Arthurian retellings are not 'dark age' sites, which are few in number anyway, but medieval castles, where one can imagine bards and minstrels regaling the nobility with tales of the Sword in the Stone, Gawain and the Green Knight, Gawain and the Loathly Lady, Tristan and Isolde, Lancelot and Guinevere, Parsifal and the Quest for the Holy Grail. At hillfort sites, which may have been briefly re-used after the departure of the Romans, earlier Arthurian legends such as 'Culhwch and Olwen' could be told. The Irish stories of Fionn Mac Cumaill, which parallel Arthur in some ways and which belong to the same period, could also be told at such sites.

Saxon Invasion It was Hengist who led the Saxon invasion of Britain in 443. The Saxon tide (the White Dragon) was, according to legend, stemmed for some decades by Arthur and his warriors (the Red Dragon), but after two hundred years Saxon settlement was complete and peace, of a sort, was achieved. Essex, Sussex and Wessex are named after the early Saxon regions, East Anglia after the territory of the Angles. Initially the Anglo-Saxon kingdoms rotated the high-kingship of England, but eventually Wessex emerged as the supreme focus of power. This was due in part to Alfred the Great who, in the ninth century, managed to turn back the Vikings when all other kingdoms had been overcome.

Alfred is the only English king to be called the 'Great'. He earned this title by, amongst other things, issuing a humane code of laws, establishing a school for the sons of the nobility, initiating the Anglo-Saxon Chronicle so his people would know about their past, and inventing a candle clock! In spite of all this there are few stories about him and no legends comparable to those of Arthur.

The paucity of Saxon legends may have something to do with the conversion of the Saxons to Christianity after the arrival of Augustine in AD 596. From that point on there was a fierce rejection of the old gods and all the mythology that went with them. The main pre-Christian Anglo-Saxon story to have survived is 'Beowulf' which is set in Denmark. This is a well crafted heroic tale of how Beowulf overcame the frightful, half-human water monster Grendel and Grendel's mother. In its detail it provides considerable insight into the life of the Saxon court, ship burials and funerary rites in the seventh century.

Another important source of information and story about the Anglo-Saxon period is the 'Ecclesiastical History of the English People', written by the Venerable Bede in Jarrow, Northumbria and spanning 800 years up to AD 731. Bede describes in detail the coming of Christianity to England and provides an eye witness account of the Synod of Whitby. He also tells the story of Caedmon, the cowherd of Whitby who, moved by divine inspiration, composed some of the first songs and poems in English, including the oldest surviving English hymn, praising 'God the Creator'. Most later Anglo-Saxon poetry shows varying degrees of Christian influence. Three well known examples - 'The Wanderer', 'The Seafarer' and 'The Ruin' - touch on the universal and timeless themes of loneliness, the struggles of the sailor against the storm and the transience of earthly joys. 'The Ruin' would be a particularly appropriate poem for an historic site.

Sites for Stories Saxon stories can be told appropriately in many places in England: for example, Old Sarum, where there was a battle in AD 552; the Saxon town of Shaftesbury; Offa's Dyke; Saxon churches and the sites of ruined Saxon villages.

Viking Invasion The Vikings set sail from Scandinavia and after rounding northern Scotland, descended on Ireland in AD 793. They were formidable warriors, fighting in battle, according to their own chroniclers, like mad wolves. Going 'beserk' is a term that derives from Viking battle frenzy. Monasteries and coastal settlements were burned and plundered mercilessly, leading to the pitiful prayer, 'Oh Lord deliver us from the fury of the Northmen.' In 853 they set up a kingdom in Ireland and used it as a base from which to raid England and Wales. Eventually they took Northumbria, Yorkshire, Norfolk and the Midlands, territory which was known as Danelaw. Little by little the fury of the Northmen abated. They settled down, became farmers and merchants, intermarried with the local population and their

Old Sarum, Wiltshire.

ENGLISH HERITAGE

children became Christians like everyone else.

The Vikings had a culture with a strong oral tradition of myths and sagas which date back to 1000 BC and which are therefore among the oldest surviving stories to have had an impact on the British Isles. Many of them were written down in the twelfth century as Icelandic sagas and their mood and atmosphere reflect the geography of that land.

They include a creation story which describes how the world was made from the body of a giant born of ice and fire; how a great cow licked the first god from the salty ice; how the sun and the moon are chased across the sky by wolves; how the universe is composed of nine worlds on three levels, Asgard, the home of the gods, Midgard, the home of humans, giants and dwarfs, and Niflheim, the home of the dead; how the great guardian ash tree, Yggdrasill, with its roots sinking down to each level, nourishes and sustains all life; how a squirrel runs up and down the tree carrying insults back and forth between a serpent in the roots and an eagle in the topmost branches. It is a vivid and complete cosmology not found in any of the other surviving pre-Christian mythologies of Britain.

In the Norse pantheon Odin (god of war and poetry), Thor (god of law and order) and Freyr (god of fertility) are the leading gods; their names survive today in three of our weekdays. The drama of the myths arises from the tension between the gods and the giants, often stirred up and complicated by the double dealing of Loki, the shape-changing trickster whose initial mischievousness turns downright evil and results in eventual world destruction in the holocaust of Ragnarok. This end proves to be a new beginning and involves the resurrection of Balder, the most merciful, gentle and loved of the gods. His death, at the hands of the deceitful Loki, is one of the most famous of all Norse tales.

Sites for Stories

Viking sites may be relatively few but the Vikings impact was far-reaching. York was the capital for Eric Blood-Axe, the Viking king, and there are sites of landings, devastations and battles, as well as more peaceful signs of settlement, in many parts of northern and eastern Britain. During this time, from AD 800 to AD 1000, their mythology was very much alive, so stories drawn from Norse myths and sagas can be validly told at any Viking site.

THE MEDIEVAL PERIOD

As a result of the spread of writing many of the pre-Christian oral traditions of Britain were, in the 12th century, written down for the first time. This secured a permanent record of at least fragments of the storytelling heritage, but it also meant the development of more literary forms which eventually replaced the living storyteller. For a while troubadors and minstrels filled the role of entertainers, performing plays with music rather than telling stories. Then, after AD 1450 and the invention of printing, books began to take over in literate circles. Though for some time they were still read out loud rather than silently, it was the beginning of the end for the bards. Our modern 'poet laureate' is all that remains of the bardic tradition. Storytelling continued, of course, but more informally amongst still illiterate folk in what might be called the 'fireside tradition'.

ENGLISH HERITAGE

The mischievous Loki reaches for mistletoe, the only thing in the world that he has not sworn never to harm to the best-loved god Balder.

Folktales

It was by the fireside in tents, huts and cottages up and down the land that folktales were told. These stories often have a medieval feel to

them, though many of their themes and characters go back to even earlier times. Talking animals are reminiscent of hunter gatherer myths; fate, fortune and fertility are farming themes many times reworked. But in folktales we don't hear about the gods, though Christian influence has given the devil a sizable part to play. And the heroes, instead of being nobles and warriors, are woodcutters, millers, beggars and fishermen. Nameless, humble folk they sometimes manage to attain a level of wisdom or good luck that elevates them to heroic status. The world of these wondertales is magical, full of little people, giants, witches, miracles and visits to the Otherworld. Often the girl or boy of lowliest origin is the one who rises to marry the prince or princess. Whatever supernatural creative power is left in these stories seems at last to have reached ordinary, yet archetypal, people.

Folktales have been filtered through many generations of tellers, and though they may seem bizarre and unbelievable to us today, they embody collective ways of making sense out of experience and contain much that is real and true. They may be magically enchanting, but they are not merely escapist entertainment. Hidden within them are the teachings of the people.

THE MASTERS AND FELLOWS OF CORPUS CHRISTI COLLEGE, CAMBRIDGE

A highland seanchaidh recites the descent of the boy King Alexander III at his inauguration at the Moot Hill of scone, 1249.

The rest is history From 1066 the historical record becomes increasingly detailed and is a good source for stories about what actually happened, at least, according to one viewpoint or another. Historical stories are quite different from myths, legends and folktales. Whereas the latter are about firing the imagination, expressing beliefs and finding satisfying answers to human questions, history is an attempt to come up with a rational account of how and why things happened. Historical narrative may lack the form and magic of oral tales, but on the other hand, fact can be stranger than fiction. What 'really' happened, told as a story, has a special dramatic appeal. Any supernatural creative power that exists in 'true' stories shifts to real people, individuals who once lived but who are now elevated to legendary status: the Black Prince, Joan of Arc, Henry VIII, Drake and Nelson to name a few. The proliferation of local legends based on historical characters and incidents illustrates this tendancy to shape and exaggerate history into story. Robin Hood is a good example.

ENGLISH HERITAGE.

Old Wardour Castle, Wiltshire.

Sites for Stories The two principle kinds of sites we have inherited from the Medieval period are castles and abbeys. They represent the two poles of medieval life, with market towns, peasant villages, forests and fields in between.

Abbeys Monasteries and abbeys usually began as pious and humble institutions, but as their abbots' taste for wealth, land and power increased so their religious purity decreased. However, saints' stories are obvious tales for telling in ruined abbeys and Bede is a good source for early ecclesiastical history. It is also possible to draw on the pre-Christian legends that were written down by industrious clerics of the time: for example, 'The Mabinogion' and Geoffrey of Monmouth's work. Chaucer's more literary 'Canterbury Tales' have the flavour of pilgrimage and carry the memory of times when stories were told. And there are folktales of monks who get into a stew over unholy appetites and abbots who do dubious deals with knights. Much is known about the daily life of abbeys and this too can be presented in story form. Last but not least is the Dissolution, a tragic ending which comes as a dramatic climax to the Abbey Tale.

Castles Castles are such classic and archetypal places in European legend and folklore that there is never any shortage of story material to be presented in them. We can imagine that they were places where Arthurian legends were told as well as some of the earlier Celtic material mentioned above. There are innumerable folktales which feature castles as dominant motifs, kings and queens as principal characters. Some of the Scottish Traveller stories are especially poignant as it is invariably the poor beggarman or old witchy woman who teaches the king a lesson in the end. And of course the evergreen legend of Robin Hood fits well in castles - and forests!

ENGLISH HERITAGE

THE ENLIGHTENMENT: 17TH and 18TH CENTURY ENGLAND

After the Civil War in the 1640's England became a more peaceful land. Fortified stone castles were no longer needed and because they were often uncomfortable and always expensive the wealthy classes began, instead, to build mansions in the country and grand houses in the towns. Rather than employing a storyteller they relied, for their entertainment, on the growing availability of romantic literature.

One of the most popular genres at this time was the fairy tale, penned by such authors as the Frenchman Charles Perrault. Many of these stories derived from the oral folktales of ordinary people. But in writing them down for a well-to-do audience they were pruned of their more 'primitive' content and adorned with figures and themes appealing to the aesthetic tastes of the elite. For example, 'Beauty and the Beast' may have originally been a fertility story in which maidens were sacrificed to appease threatening giants or dragons. The transformed fairy tale takes place in a grand mansion and the ugly beast eventually becomes a saviour who, as a handsome prince, rewards the virtues of industry, obedience and humility. Thus the story shows evidence of careful crafting for a specific end. For, whereas folktales were retold by generations of storytellers and evolved unconsciously, fairy tales were created consciously by individual authors. They were intended to be read by a particular audience and deliberately promoted certain values and social norms.

During these centuries the frontiers of the world known to Europeans were being expanded rapidly by voyages of exploration and discovery. Travellers' tales, real and imaginary, were therefore also very popular forms of literature. Not only was there the adventure of the journey to recount, but also the encounter with 'exotic' peoples. In time some of the myths and legends from these other cultures filtered back to Britain and became a subject of interest in the drawing rooms of the literati.

Sites for Stories Fairy tales are fitting to tell in the mansions and manor houses of town and country, but there are folktales too - especially those that feature the lord of the manor, like 'Clever Gretel' or 'The Cook and the Heron' - which would be suitable as well. Historical stories and legendary history, appropriate to location and period, would make good telling in the mansions, and in the merchant houses of town and city, traveller's tales would suit. In such places it might even be legitimate to include stories drawn from other cultures of the world. Indeed, it seems right that stories told at more recent 'historic sites' should reflect the multi-cultural nature of British society today. They are the newest leaves on the great 'Tree of Tales'.

Maiden Castle, Dorset.

PREPARING FOR A STORYTELLING VISIT

PREPARATION FOR TEACHERS

Initial Research The first step in preparing for a visit to an historic site is to become acquainted with the period your particular site represents and then, by reading the guide book, teachers' handbook (if available), and any other site-specific information, to become familiar with the site itself. At this stage it is also wise to be thinking about the issues and themes you want to explore in your stories.

First Visit It is essential for you to visit the site before taking the children. Explore the ruins at your own pace, soaking up the atmosphere, finding what interests you and trying to imagine how it was when the place was inhabited. Also look out for appropriate, sheltered spots to pause and tell a story. This is a creative and often intuitive process and you may find that the best route for you is not the one visitors usually take. If they have time question the custodian closely for titbits of information and story. By the time you finish this recce be clear of your probable route, the probable stopping places and the story themes you want to present on your visit with the children.

Historical Background On any visit to an historic site it is important to give some historical background. This is true with a storytelling approach as well. Your introduction to the children should include essential facts about when and why the place was built, how, by whom and what happened there. Ideally this introduction should be woven together as a story, inviting the children in and making them want to know more. For example, in introducing Avebury:

'This is the largest stone circle in the world. It was built about 5000 years ago by the early farmers of Britain. They moved these sarsen stones from those hills, probably with the help of teams of oxen. The ditches, which were twice as deep as they are now, were dug using antlers as

ENGLISH HERITAGE

A planning visit is essential to learn about the site and where you want to tell stories.

picks and ox's shoulder blades for shovels. Avebury could well have been an important religious centre for the people of southern Britain. For example it is possible that great ceremonies were carried out here to celebrate the return of spring.'

At the end of the visit it may also be appropriate to provide further factual information about how the place came to be abandoned, what it was that led to its present ruinous state. For example:

'In the seventeenth century many people associated Avebury with the devil and some of the stones were pulled down. They were broken up and used to build houses in the village of Avebury. One man, a barber or a dentist, was trying to 'extract' one of the stones when it fell and killed him. His skeleton was found when the circle was restored to its present condition.'

Following this approach the programme comes to be shaped like a sandwich: it begins with some historical background, proceeds with a tasty filling of myth, legend or folktale and concludes with an explanation of why the site was abandoned and perhaps something about its history as a ruin.

Time Travel Storytellers often use a phrase like 'Once upon a time...' or 'We are leaving our time now...' to facilitate an imaginative shift to another time. We have found that the song 'Let's go back in time' (see page 34) is enjoyable for the children to sing, functions as a 'time song' ('we can't afford a time machine!') and also gives them a sense of how far back they are going: 'To the time of our grandfather's grandfather's...etc... grandfather!" There is a simple verse that needs to be composed for each site. At the end of your visit you should change the words to: *'Let's come back in time'* in order to return to the present. Learning the song can be part of the children's preparation for the visit.

Creating Atmosphere Having 'gone back in time' it is helpful to create an impression of what you would be seeing, hearing, smelling and feeling when the place was in its heyday. This could be in the form of 'a day in the life of...' For example, at the gateway to a courtyard house in a Celtic village:

'People rise at dawn and have a breakfast of gruel and perhaps last night's leftovers. The courtyard is swept clean, the great wooden gates are opened and out come the squawking chickens and yelping dogs. Most people have got work to do. Some will be ploughing and sowing in the fields or panning for tin in the streams or looking after the animals. Others stay here to spin and weave, tan skins or make tools. Once a week two men go down to the coast with a packhorse to trade wool and tin for fish. At the end of the day everyone comes back here. The cows and pigs are brought into their byres and the gates are closed. There are wild boars and wolves in those forests you know. When darkness has closed in and everyone's had their fill from the cauldron someone will sit back and ask for a story...'

Or it could be the description of a special occasion, such as entering into the castle kitchen on the day of a great feast:

'Today a great feast is being prepared. The pile of loaves on that table are fresh from the bakery. Below the great chimney

breast are huge ovens and a spit for roasting pork or venison. On that wall are hanging stockpots and basting pans and a cauldron big enough to contain fifty portions. Watch out for the table with the chopping block. Those knives and cleavers are sharp! Hanging from the iron hooks screwed into the oak beams are joints of meat, sacks of wheat, cleaning cloths and several brace of pheasants. On the floor is a layer of sawdust, freshly spread every morning. It's very busy today, and the heat from the fires and steam from the pots is making the cooks and scullions sweat. When the food is ready it's passed through the hatch into the servery and the maids take it up to the great hall. I expect after the feast the lord will call his storyteller...'

This kind of scene setting will help to bring the site to life and create a context for telling a story. Historical novelists can help you to imagine such scenes. Sometimes even guidebooks will too!

Music and dance at Restormel Castle, Cornwall.

ENGLISH HERITAGE

Choosing the Stories
This can be the most challenging part of the preparation. Refer to the chapter on 'The Tree of Tales' to find the kind of story appropriate to your site. Listen to stories on the accompanying tape. Also see the chapter on 'Improving your storytelling'. The key points to remember are:

■ only tell stories you enjoy and want to tell

■ be sure that the story has a meaningful link to the site

■ you will probably need three to five stories; look for variety and balance; if possible, make connections between the stories so they weave together into a larger whole

■ the telling time may range from a few minutes to more than half an hour; longer stories can be divided into parts and told in several locations

■ practise your stories beforehand, even if only to an audience of one.

Music and Dance
Moving from one part of the site to another can be enhanced by using music, Pied Piper fashion. This may be simply the beating of a drum but can also include recorder, flute or any other portable instrument a teacher or pupil can play. If possible

involve the children in making this music, being sure to practise it beforehand. At the end of a story it is good to have a few moments of stillness before moving off to the next location. In these moments a fragment of tune on an ocarina or a whistle can be an atmospheric way of rounding off the tale. Some stories lend themselves to a musical accompaniment, which will also need to be rehearsed prior to the visit.

Stories involve the imaginative participation of children, but for balance it is as well to engage them physically at times as well. The best way to do this is through dance. For most of the earlier historic sites the circle dance is a good form. It is not difficult to choreograph an effective dance by beginning with a circle holding hands and then combining steps or skips to the left and right, turns, bows, jumps, movements in and out of the centre and spirals. Variations can include miming animals and even enacting the agricultural cycle of sowing and growing, harvesting, grinding and eating. These dances can be accompanied by a simple drum beat, though a tune on a whistle or recorder will add to the effect. Dancing in castles is likely to be more courtly, with lines facing each other, bowing to partners and so on. Country dancing is a useful source for ideas on this. See Resources for books on dancing with children. Again it is worth practising the dances before making the visit.

Costumes, masks, props
It may help you to switch from the role of teacher to storyteller by using costume. This need not be elaborate. It doesn't even have to relate to the period of your site. Indeed, a complete medieval minstrel's outfit may distract, rather than enhance, attention. Something

simple like a hat or a shawl may be sufficient. Donning an unusual garment or adding colour to your normal appearance will signal: 'Hello, I'm a storyteller.' Of course, if you wish to get carried away, then do! Some abbeys have a complete set of monks' habits for use by a class and teachers. This is too good an opportunity to miss, as all the children can become erstwhile novices.

A further step for the incurably dramatic is introduce characters into the storytelling. For example, a character from the story can be brought to life by using a mask. The character can then tell some of the tale from his or her point of view. Bringing the cook into a story involving a king and a kitchen boy will give a different, and perhaps amusing, perspective on the situation. Another possibility if there is more than one storyteller is for one to play the part of someone who lived at the site. That person could then tell stories in character.

Sometimes it can also be useful to use props. A horn for signalling and a basket for carrying instruments are obvious examples. One of the most spellbinding occasions was when, at a site where people used to work tin, one of the storytellers whipped out a blow torch, melted some pewter in a tiny crucible, poured it into a mold cut from cuttlefish and made a beautiful, shiny brooch. The children were amazed. Thinking laterally can provide exciting ways of complementing the storytelling and reaching across the curriculum.

Contingencies
If it looks like rain be prepared with waterproofs and have a roofed alternative in mind. Many sites have no education centres or even spaces to shelter out of the rain. Barns and even workman's mess huts have been conscripted in such circumstances!

PREPARATION FOR CHILDREN

On Storytelling The more children are steeped in storytelling and the history and stories of the period, the more they will benefit from the site visit.

Here are two exercises to develop children's awareness of, and skill at, storytelling. Further ideas for exploring stories and storytelling can be found in 'Becoming a Storyteller' and 'Playing with Storytelling' later in the book.

Telling stories: Our Own

■ Explain that although writing was invented about 3000 years ago, in Britain until about 500 years ago it was mainly only monks and clerics who could read and write. Books were first printed in 1450, but even 150 years ago most people were still illiterate. They passed their knowledge on by talking to each other and telling stories. In fact that's how knowledge has always been passed on from parents to children from the beginning of time.

■ Explain that we still tell stories, and give some examples, such as...when I fell off my bike, what happened on holiday, how the pet budgie escaped, when I got lost in the city, my uncle who saw a ghost, the fire that nearly burnt down the school, the argument I had with my best friend...

■ Ask each child to think of a story about something he or she

to to make them into funnier or more exciting stories? Ask them to did or that happened to them recently. Ask them to: 'Go over it in your mind once or twice. If you like, make a note of the main points. Then, in pairs, tell your story to your partner. Swap round and listen to your partners story.'

■ After they have tried this explain that people often EXAGGERATE what happened to them to make it into a BETTER STORY. 'I wasn't lost I was kidnapped!' 'It wasn't just a pound coin it was gold and treasure!' 'Budgie? It was like a wild eagle!' 'He was a real giant!' 'It was a human skeleton and it started to move!' However, no matter how much exaggeration there has to remain the germ of something 'true'.

■ So ask them to think about their stories again. How could they be exaggerated or changed or added

try out the new, improved story on another partner. Then they can tell their partner's story back to them, exaggerating it even more!

■ Finally explain that this is the way stories change as they pass by word of mouth from one generation to the next. It is the way personal stories grow into myths, legends and folktales.

■ There is an Irish idea that if a story is told three times is becomes a 'traditional tale'. On the first telling someone says: 'This happened to me the other day...' The second time it becomes: 'I met this man and he said...' The third time it is simply: 'There was this man...' In other words, if the story is universal enough still to be told when there is no knowledge of the original person, then it 'goes into the tradition'. Not many stories survive that process.

Telling stories: From Books

This exercise is to give children the opportunity to learn to tell a story they have read in a book.

■ Explain that today, apart from stories about ourselves, our families and friends, most stories we know come from books or television. Ask the children to think of a story they know from a book. Perhaps they read it or perhaps someone read it to them. How well can they remember it?

■ Explain that once we have read a story we often forget large parts of it. Perhaps we think we can always go back to the book. We do not remember it well enough to

tell someone else. In the old days people listened to the same story many times. Some of them also had very good memories.

■ Ask the children to choose a short story from a book they like. Make sure it has plenty of action, just a few characters and not too much description. Read it once then think it through in your minds, seeing the main scenes in pictures. Make a 'cartoon strip' of the story with, say, twelve frames, each frame with a caption. This means the whole movement of the tale can be seen in miniature. Then read it again, filling in the gaps. Some bits, like the speech,

may need to be learned by heart.

■ In pairs ask them to tell their story to their partner. They listen to their partner's story. Afterwards they can check the original story again, filling in the missing bits. Now repeat the exercise telling the story to someone else.

■ Encourage them to tell their story to as many people as they can: parents, younger brothers and sisters, children in another class, the postman...anyone who will listen. After a while, you can say to them, 'You'll find that the story has become your story. You will always have it with you wherever you go!'

The Clearing and the Cave
Find a story about an animal that talks and helped human beings. This is one of the very oldest kinds of stories. Look at examples of cave paintings. Try to do a similar picture to illustrate your story.

Stone Circles and Burial Chambers
Make up a story about how our ancestors discovered farming. Find a story that they told about the gods and goddesses. Find, or make up, a story about the seasons of the year, about why, after the harvest there is always the cold and dark of winter followed by the new life of spring.

Hut Circles and Hillforts
Look for legends about Celtic heroes or heroines, perhaps one from Ireland (Cu Culann or Finn MacCool) and one from Wales (Bran or Culhwch). Find out about the bards. Make up a bardic poem to celebrate a king or queen. Look for the story of Taliesin, the primary chief bard of Wales.

Roman Remains
Find a story from ancient Roman or Greek mythology. Now find an historical story about what happened when the Romans came to Britain (Caradog's Last Stand, the Revolt of Boudica). What are the differences between the two? Which do you like better? Try to imagine the stories the Celts would have told about the visits to Britain by Julius Caesar.

Holy Wells and Monasteries
Read some stories about early British saints (Patrick, Bridget, Columba, Cuthbert, Wilfrid, David, Illtud, George) and their miracles. What do people think of their miracles today? Is there anyone alive now who might be called a saint? Learn your favourite saint's story.

Saxon Halls, Viking ships
Listen to the story of 'Beowulf'. Find out about Caedmon and look for some early poems in English. Which days of the week are named after Norse gods? Find out a story about them. What is the meaning of the other weekday names? What is the story of Loki, the mischief making trickster god and Balder, the gentlest and best loved of the gods?

Medieval Castles
Stories about King Arthur and the Knights of the Round Table were probably told by storytellers in the old castles. Find one of these stories to tell ('The Sword in the Stone', 'Sir Gawaine and the Loathly Lady'). There are many folktales with kings and queens living in castles. Find such a story to tell ('The Happy Man's Shirt', 'I love you more than salt'). We also know what really happened at some castles. Find a true, historical story about a castle.

Mansions and Manor Houses
Find a fairy tale to tell in a well-to-do mansion. A ghost story is a spooky idea too. In a manor or merchant house think of a traveller's tale to tell. And what about a story from another culture across the sea?

AFTER THE VISIT: WRITTEN WORK

Amplifying a Scene
Children choose a scene and try to imagine it as fully as they can with their eyes closed. Encourage them to imaginatively see, hear, smell and touch details which were not in the original telling. The story may become more contemporary. Now write a paragraph on a page about that particular scene of the story, incorporating the new elements. The page can then be illustrated, and, if all the scenes of the story are covered, all the pages can be bound together in the right order as a book.

Make up a Poem
Based on their experience of the day at the site, make up a poem about going back in time and being there when the place was inhabited. This can be done individually or as a whole class making up a group poem. For example, after a visit to Oswestry hillfort a group of juniors wrote this poem:

When the Battle is Over
Steep ramparts circling around
ten acres of bumpy Celtic ground.
The whole world stretches
away -
green fields, silver streams,
busy roads, dark forests,
the flat land of the Shropshire
plains
and towering mountains to the
west.
The cold air makes me feel
uneasy.
I know I am standing on a place
a warrior stood
two thousand years ago.
The feel never goes.
Out of the silence I hear
the sounds of laughter,
posts being hammered into the
ground,
a wolf howling in the quiet night
air.
Out of the haze out see
a spiral of smoke in the middle of
a circle of people,
they're telling stories, singing.
Someone is washing blood from
a spear,
glad the battle is over,
glad to see the backs of men
returning to their families.
The haze disappears
and I am left standing alone
on the ruins of old Oswestry
hillfort.

Writing 'a day in the life of' story:
this works especially well written in the first person immediately after the dramatic exploration of life at the site described above. In the absence of a drama it can be based simply on the experience of the visit to the site itself.

■ See 'Playing with Storytelling' page 31 for further ideas on working stories.

On History Background history of the period to which the site belongs can be drawn from the chapter on 'The Tree of Tales'. Site specific history will need to come from guide books, teachers' handbooks and local history books. The children can be involved in this research prior to your site visit.

On Stories As part of the research for stories of your site's period the activity (TOP LEFT OPPOSITE) suggestions for the children may be helpful.

The Day Itself Providing the preparations are complete and there is a good balance between story, explanation, moving around the site, music and dance, the main thing to remember is to enjoy yourselves. It is important to have a well planned structure, but it is good not to be too rigid in adhering to your plan. Flexibility will allow for spontaneity and surprise, two key ingredients for the working of magic. And magic has to be part of the brew when we are travelling imaginatively in time!

If the day is a success, it would seem a shame only to do it once. A few more times and you could really perfect it. So why not offer your services to other classes within the school, or even other local schools. You will be developing your own experience and also spreading the word about storytelling at historic sites!

Chysauster Ancient Village, Cornwall.

ENGLISH HERITAGE

AFTER THE VISIT: ORAL WORK

Retelling the Stories

Retelling stories is not a rote exercise but a very creative act. It works best to have a retelling session within a day of hearing the stories.

Divide the class into small groups and give each group a story to retell. Let them go round the group, taking it in turns to tell part of the story. This way, if someone forgets then someone else will probably remember, and between them they will recall the whole story.

Now let them work in pairs with someone from another group. The partners take it in turns to tell their story to each other. And then they can try telling the story they've just heard back to the person who told them. In this way they are gradually coming to know and be able to tell two stories.

The process can continue, theoretically, until everyone can tell all the stories. It is important to encourage the children to tell the stories to other people outside their class, as they may have done with the earlier exercises.

Dramatically Exploring a Story

Children naturally like to play-act, and the storytelling may quickly develop into acting out. It is important not to skip the storytelling stage, as this is very valuable in developing oracy skills. But it is equally important to allow the impulse for drama its opportunity for expression. Initially the story can be performed as a series of cartoon frames, with characters frozen like statues, representing the various scenes. Then it can be acted out more conventionally with characters playing the parts and a narrator.

Dramatically Exploring the Site

Storytelling can also be incorporated into a wider drama that explores life at the site when it was inhabited. This is not the place for a detailed description of a drama lesson. However the following steps provide one method of working which may be useful:

■ Do a range of physical warm up activities which get the children moving and practising in mime some of the skills that will be needed in playing roles and characters.

■ Choose groups of children to enact the different roles that are taken by people as they go about their work. Be sure they are clear about their tasks. Some individuals may be needed to take on such key roles as lord, messenger, mother, thief.

■ Set the scene by describing in detail the sights, sounds, smells and time of day. Find a way of bringing the children into their roles: for example, as the day begins they wake up and go about their work.

■ As the scene develops move about, in role yourself, prompting and challenging, finding out what is going on, making sure everyone knows what they are doing. At some point a snatch of story could be told. Then, when it is least expected introduce a surprise for example news of the approach of the king; the discovery of a theft or a dead body...!

■ Through improvisation allow the drama to develop. It may reach a clear conclusion or it may need to be stopped at an appropriate moment. In that case, freeze the action and go round asking each child, in role, what they are feeling and thinking. Find a satisfying ending, a way of bringing them back to the present.

BECOMING A STORYTELLER

WHY TELL TALES?

Reading stories aloud from books will always play a part in education. But it is not storytelling. Telling is older than reading (or being read to) and is a more complete form of communication. It has neither the careful polish of literature nor the rehearsed spectacle of drama. Instead it is a unique form of improvisation created in the moment through the interplay of audience, storyteller and story. This makes the told tale alive and immediate in a way which compels both listener and teller alike. It is not lifted from a dry page, but comes from within the teller, and so seems to be the teller's own tale - as if he or she were there at the time. It is received by the audience as a direct and personal gift from the storyteller.

A *story reader* repeats the words written on a page, and so is limited by the text and can only afford brief glances at the listeners. But a *storyteller* can have almost continuous eye contact with an audience and has the freedom to respond to their mood. The pace, emphasis and detail of a story can be different each time, making telling a creative and quite intimate act.

It has also been observed that the act of storytelling raises the language level of the storyteller. As a result storytellers display a confidence and power that is not present in their other uses of language. Storytelling is therefore an effective way of improving oral fluency. It is good for teachers and children.

CHOOSING A STORY

In the past we would have told only stories we had heard. Now, notwithstanding the storytelling revival, few of us are able to tap directly into an oral tradition. We have to rely on books. One advantage of this is that we can draw on almost any cultural tradition we choose in selecting a story. However it does mean reading many stories before we find one we like and want to tell. When we find it, usually we know.

In seeking stories suitable for historic sites one is constrained by the period and the availability of stories. It is not always possible to meet all the criteria. However, the characteristics of a good story include:

■ an inviting beginning that gets straight into the action

■ a clear and well developed plot

■ a few believable, though perhaps unusual, characters

■ a problem, dilemma or conflict that comes in early on and creates suspense

■ plenty of action building to a climax

■ incidents related in word pictures that evoke vivid images in the listener's mind

■ no superfluous explanation or description

■ an edge of excitement, which can include fear or sadness

■ pleasing sounds, repeated phrases and rhythms which can involve the audience

■ an ending - perhaps surprising - which resolves the problem in a satisfying way

Clearly the most important criterion is that you like the story and want to tell it.

LEARNING TO TELL A STORY

Be Yourself When telling a story, be yourself. Do not try to become a dramatic character or something you're not.

Knowlton Earthworks, Dorset.

ENGLISH HERITAGE

Off the Page When stories are written down they may gain a certain refinement but they lose the raw vitality of the living word. So to lift a story off the page and make it live again requires some practice.

Not by heart Stories from the oral tradition - myths, legends and folktales - do not need to be learned word for word. That approach may be necessary for tales finely crafted by literary authors, but the old stories are best told in a tellers own words. That does not mean there is no memorising to do, but you should aim for a feeling of spontaneity rather than recitation. However there will be key phrases, rhymes and apt descriptions that you will need to learn verbatim. It is specially important to be confident with beginnings and endings.

Different approaches It takes time and practice to make a story your own, so it is important to allow that time. Some people learn best by visualising the story as a series of moving pictures in their imaginations. Others have a more auditory approach, preferring to listen to tape recordings of the story and concentrating on the sound and rhythm of the language. Yet others like to write the story down, sometimes in simple outline, occasionally in considerable detail. All of these methods have their value and can, of course, be used in combination.

Grasping the plot Obviously the first step is to read the story through several times. Decide on what you like most about the story that you want to convey to your audience - its humour, sense of wonder, magical strangeness, the way it moves you, its beauty or wisdom. Become familiar with its basic construction, noticing how the dramatic tension is introduced, how it builds to a climax and resolves in the ending. This might be a good time to jot down an outline of the story and characters and then to go back to the original to fill the gaps in your memory.

Seeing the story Get to know the people and settings of the story by imagining them in as much detail as possible. This can be done by closing your eyes and visualing a scene from the story, using all the senses to make it alive and real. Then, in your imagination, walk through the scene until you meet one of the story's characters. Notice the clothes, the gait, the facial expressions, how the person talks. In this way you'll learn more about the tale than is written in the text. Only when you can see the story vividly yourself can you make your audience see it.

Timing is the essence As you go through the story in your mind you'll become aware of what words to emphasise, where to pause, where to accelerate, where to slow down. Timing is crucially important in any dramatic delivery, especially storytelling. Some climaxes have more impact delivered slowly, others are better speeded up. Remember, don't be afraid to pause.

Practicing the story, playing with your voice Once you have got this far you are ready to try your story out on anyone who will listen. An audience of one is enough. Alternatively you can try it out into a tape recorder. After this first telling go back to your original source to find out what you left out. With more tellings your timing will improve and you'll discover ways of modulating your voice. By varying volume, pitch, breathing and speed you'll be able to create a wide range of characters and moods.

Movement and gesture Also in the telling you'll probably find yourself using gestures. Painting hand pictures in the air can add considerably to the enjoyment of a story, but beware of being distracting. Some storytellers move their bodies a great deal in their telling, adding to the drama. Others barely move their mouths. Gesture and movement are not essential for the telling of a good story, but they can add to the effect. Clearly it is a matter for each individual storyteller to decide.

Old Wardour Castle, Wiltshire.

Eric Maddern and Kathie Prince at Avebury, Wiltshire.

THE TWO PICKPOCKETS

What follows here is an example of a story broken down into its 'essentials' (perhaps eight sentences); each essential being described visually; the standard bits being extracted from the original; overall giving a sense of a story being deconstructed and then reconstructed for telling.

There once lived a pickpocket, a master thief. He could take the wallet from your pocket or the purse from your hand-bag without letting you feel a thing.

Well, one day this pickpocket was walking along an empty street, it was early on a Sunday morning, the city where he operated was deserted. He turned a corner, and then, suddenly, he saw walking towards him, a beautiful woman. Something about her smile, and something about it being a Sunday conspired to make him think better of his natural reflex, and he thrust his hands deep into his own pockets and walked past her.

But he hadn't walked far when he became aware of a strange lightness in his own pocket, his left breast pocket, he felt it and realised that his own wallet was gone. He turned and ran back to the woman:

'Excuse me, I'm not going to call the police or anything, but tell me, did you just take my wallet?'

The woman blushed and lowered her eyes:

'Well, as it happens, yes I did.'

'That was fantastic, I thought I was good, but that was brilliant. Listen, why don't you and me go into business together, between the two of us we could clean up the whole town?'

The woman thought about it, and she agreed, and they went into business together, and it wasn't long before they were both stinking rich. And as often happens if a man and a woman find themselves in a close partnership, they fell in love.

Well, one thing led to another and they were married, and then, a few months later she discovered that she was pregnant. They were delighted, with his genes and her chromosomes, this baby would grow up to be the greatest thief ever to have lived! Nine months passed, and at last the labour pains began, the midwife was fetched and the baby was born.

It was a fine strapping boy, but the pickpocket and his wife couldn't hide their disappointment, for one of the baby's arms was curled up against his chest, and his little fingers were knotted tight. With only one arm how could he ever be the greatest thief in the world?

They took the child to one specialist after another, and their money was soon all spent, nobody could do a thing. Then finally, as a last resort, they thought they'd try a dowser. The dowser was an old woman, she took the baby and laid it on a table. Then she took a thread of cotton, with a little piece of pure gold at the end of it, and she suspended it over the child's arm and began to ask questions, watching to see whether the gold swung clockwise or widdishins.

But when the baby saw that piece of gold swinging above his head, his eyes lit up as they'd never lit up before, and slowly his little arm began to reach up towards it, and slowly his little fingers began to uncurl.

And suddenly, out of his hand fell the midwife's wedding ring!

This little folktale is popular with storytellers, many of whom tell their own version of it.

In order to tell a story you have to be able to 'see' it, you have to 'make it your own'.

The best way of seeing a story is to first reduce it to its essentials - to its skeleton - then to rebuild it, flesh out the skeleton in your own way, with your own words.

With this tale the skeleton might look like this:

■ A pickpocket notices his own wallet is missing

■ He discovers the culprit is a beautiful girl

■ They go into business together, with great success

■ They marry, she becomes pregnant, surely the child will be a master thief!

■ The child is born deformed, arm bent to chest, fist clenched

■ One specialist after another - no cure

■ The child notices something golden

■ He reaches up, opens hand......midwife's wedding ring

Now, leave the original text behind, and construct pictures, in your mind's eye, one of each section of the story. For section one you might ask yourself where the pickpocket is operating, is it a place you know? Is it a contemporary story, if not when is it set? Who is he, can you base him on someone you've seen? What's his reaction when he discovers the wallet is missing? Construct a world, a milieu in which the story is taking place. Do the same thing for the rest of the story. Reconstruct it in your own way. Much of the detail and information you won't use in the telling, but it will inform the telling.

When you've done that: found the skeleton and fleshed it out, there is a final ingredient to add - the rhythm. It's the rhythm that give life to the flesh and bones: the heart-beat of the story. At this point it's a good idea to try telling the story to a tape-recorder, or someone you know. Are there places where the story needs to move faster? Are there details that you could dwell on for longer?

Play with the telling, it'll be different every time. 'The Two Pickpockets', of course, is a simple story, but the same process is just as useful for longer, more complicated tales. Sometimes there may be passages that need to be kept intact from the original text (rhyming refrains for example), write these down alongside the skeleton. Discard the rest of the text (however much sympathy you feel for it, you can return to it later if needs be, but first of all 'make the story your own'.

Traditional stories are living things. Their proper place is between people, living on tongues and in memories, not locked in dusty volumes on library shelves. The more of them we can set free, the better!

PLAYING WITH STORYTELLING

Storytelling requires three elements: the audience, the storyteller and the story. To improve appreciation of stories and the capacity to tell stories it is worth exploring and experimenting with all three ingredients, which can be summarised as: listening, telling, the stories themselves. Here are some examples of exercises that can be done with children or teachers.

Exercises for listening

Good listening helps you, as an audience member, to enjoy a story to the full: it also helps to give the storyteller confidence.

■ **Listening to Sounds:** Sit in silence with your eyes closed and listen to the sounds of your breathing and your body. After a while switch your attention to sounds in the room, noticing them as they arise and disappear. A few minutes later become aware of sounds that are coming from outside the room. Then slowly, step by step, move your attention back to your breath. Now concentrate your attention on listening to every sound as it arises, regardless of where it comes from.

■ **Going for a Sound Walk:** Go for a walk out of the classroom, paying attention purely to the sounds that you hear - traffic, footsteps, dogs barking, conversation, birds, concrete mixers. On returning to the classroom describe the walk by using voices to re-create the sounds heard along the way.

■ **Listening to a Partner:** Get into pairs, A and B. For three minutes A talks to B about anything. B listens to A, encouraging but not interrupting. It helps if B looks directly at A, perhaps even leaning slightly towards them. When A has finished B repeats back, in summary form, what A has said. Then switch roles and repeat the process. Afterwards, talk about what it was like to listen and to be listened to.

Exercises for telling

Vocal Expression The voice is the storyteller's primary instrument; words are the notes. The voice is capable of an extraordinary range of volume, pitch, pace and tone. By playing with these variables one can create many vocal

Old Sarum, Wiltshire.

ENGLISH HERITAGE

qualities, from a nervous whisper to a shrill cry or a grumbly growl. Anyone can improve their voice, no matter where they start.

■ Begin by stretching and stimulating the muscles of the face, throat, mouth, lips, tongue and jaw; by yawning, by making bizarre faces, by poking the tongue out in all directions, by pouting the lips, by exaggerating natural expressions, by massaging the face, jaw, temples and scalp. Make a fool of yourself. Discover new possibilities.

■ Explore the range of vowel sounds, from 'oo' to 'oh' to 'or' to 'o' (as in 'odd') to 'ah' (as in 'ask') to 'a' (as in 'add') and finally, putting them all together in 'ow'. Move between the vowels with an 'm' or a 'w' at the beginning of each one. Explore the 'ee' vowel by saying 'yee' over and over again. Feel a buzzing sound spreading from the back of the throat to the neck and head. Make sounds with others just using vowels. Experiment with harmonies.

■ Consonants cut up the open ended vowels to make the rhythms of speech. Notice the difference between voiced and unvoiced consonants. Make rhythmic patterns using various consonants: e.g. k, k k, k k, k k; g, g g, g g, g g; p, p p, p p, p p; b, b b, b b, b b; t, t t, t t, t t; d, d d, d d, d d.Go for a clear and precise consonant sound. Try a sound improvisation combining vowels and consonants.

■ With a partner have a conversation in gibberish. Which emotions can be communicated through nonsense language? The extremes may be easy. Experiment with the more subtle differences between, for example, cheerfulness and clowning around, pity and sorrow, whining and agony!

■ Take a line from the speech of a story character and say it over and over again, varying the volume, pitch, pace, tone and 'breathiness' of the voice. How do each of these factors influence the nature of the character? Repeat the exercise with different characters.

■ Practise making the sound effects you might use in a story: like splashing water, a giant's footsteps, closing a door, various animal noises.

Gesture and Movement Movement and gesture (including facial expression) are the storyteller's secondary instruments. Between them they can add emphasis, vitality, illustration, humour or meaning to a storytelling.

■ Notice how a storyteller already uses gestures and encourage him or her to be bolder and more confident with them.

■ Make up a sign language to communicate a simple story without words. Find out about sign languages for the deaf. Some are both aesthetic and dramatic. Learn to tell a story using some of these signs.

■ Choose a story and, with a group, act it out in movement, mime and with sound effects. Now tell the story, using some of the movements in the telling.

Memory and Visualisation The ability to remember is obviously important to a storyteller. Memory is often improved when associated with visual images, so the capacity to visualise (or imagine) is also very valuable.

Stories tend to lodge well in the memory. One could almost say that they were designed for that purpose. Stories are memorable because they usually have a coherent structure where one thing leads to the next; thus they hang together as a whole, providing a meaningful pattern with beginning, middle and end. Often they make an impression by touching our emotions.

whether by amusing, horrifying or moving us. Good stories also create pictures in our mind. And they have simple yet exaggerated characters who are frequently found in recognisable situations. Some stories are given a musical lift by the use of rhythm and repetition. All these factors make a story vivid and memorable.

■ Sit comfortably, close your eyes and relax. Imagine being outside your home. Look at it closely, noticing the colour and texture of the walls, the position and shape of the windows, the design and material of the door. What is the door handle like? Open the door and walk inside the house. What room are you in? Notice the walls, furniture, lights, floor coverings. How do you feel there? Go to the room you know best and look around. Pick up an object. Is it hard or soft, hot or cold?

What colour and shape is it? Does it smell? Get to know this object using all your senses. How well can you remember your room?

■ Recall an experience you had. Choose one where you felt something strongly. In a relaxing position bring the incident into focus, thinking about how you will tell it as a story. Decide where to begin, what is the body of the story and where to end. Visualise in detail the scene(s) where the event took place. Remember the changing emotions you felt. Run through the sequence of events in your mind. Notice what you want to emphasise, how you might even exaggerate to improve the story. What will you leave out? Jot down brief notes to help remember the story bones. Then tell it to someone else. Later, having told the story a few times, you may wish to write it down.

■ There are numerous variations on this exercise. Essentially the group sits comfortably with eyes closed while the leader guides them on an imaginary journey. For example: 'Walk around a garden you know until you find a big tree with a door in its trunk. Open the door and enter. In a dim light you see steps and follow them down until you reach a dark lake where a boat is moored. You climb into the boat and float away. A stream carries you through black caverns and out into the daylight.The landscape around you is alive with bright birds, flowers, insects and magic. You disembark and walk along a path which takes you through a wood and up a hill to a hut. Sitting there is an old man or woman who has been expecting you. You ask questions and listen to the answers. As you are leaving you are given a gift. You walk back down the hill, through the woods and to the river. After climbing into the boat you float back to the present.'

Draw a picture illustrating scenes, feelings or moments from the journey. Afterwards talk to a partner about your picture.

■ Choose a folktale that you like. Read it through twice and then, with eyes closed, imagine the first scene. See it in detail, using all your senses. Walk through the scene until you meet the first character. Now, in your imagination, follow the whole story from beginning to end, visualising it all the way as vividly as possible. Check the original to see if you've made any major omissions. It may help to make a note of the main images of the story.

Exercises for stories
Making Up Stories Most of us are capable of creating far more from our imaginations than we would expect. These games are fun to play and add to our fund of story ideas.

■ In a circle someone starts to tell a story. Each person adds a sentence in turn and the story moves round. You may need to suggest sticking to a few characters, staying with the story's thread and working towards a climax and an ending.

■ Similar to the above except that first person begins with 'fortunately...', the next with 'unfortunately....' This way the story veers back and forth between good luck and bad.

■ Each small group has five objects (e.g. spoon, broom, scissors, basket, matchbox) which they have to make up a story about. This can be done with photographs or pictures cut from newspapers and magazines.

■ Write a list of key folktale words (e.g. forest, horse, giant, cave, spell, cauldron, fire, wolf, moon, castle, cottage, dragon, sword...) on cards and place them face down in the middle of the group. Each person takes one card and spends two or three minutes writing down their associations with that word. Repeat this with a second and third card. Then, using the ideas stimulated by the three keywords, make up a story. This can be written in note form and then told, or written out in full and then read.

■ Work with a partner. 'A' begins to spontaneously tell a story. After a couple of sentences 'B' throws in a word totally unrelated to 'A's story. 'A' has to use

that word in the story without losing the thread or pausing too long. 'B' continues to throw tricky words into 'A's' story. After a few minutes switch round. Repeat the exercise with other partners. Can be hard at first but improves with practice. Very good for spontaneity.

■ Find a sturdy twig or bent stick. Either make up a story or choose a story that you know. This works specially well with nature theme stories. Onto your stick tie or fasten bits of wool, shell, feather, leaf, stone, clay, metal or cloth etc. to stand for the scenes, characters and plot of the story. In this way the 'story stick' is both a mnemonic for the story and a creative illustration of it.

Stretching Stories The more we experiment with and explore the stories we know, the more pleasure we get from them and the more we can give to their telling.

■ Explore different ways of beginning the same story. For example, try to intrigue, shock, amuse or lead astray your listeners at the start. You may seek a response (e.g. 'Anyone ever been to the seaside?'); or you may evoke an atmosphere - spooky, playful, heroic - in your opening lines.

■ Choose and tell a story to a small group. Divide the story into sections and allocate one part for each person. Retell the story as a group, initially in the right order, then in a mixed up and random order. Try and make the story hang together even though it's told in the 'wrong' way.

■ Retell a story from the point of view of a character, or object, in it; for

example, the beans in Jack and the Beanstalk.

■ Make up a different story about a character from a story you know well.

Rhythm and Pace of Stories It is often said that timing is everything for a performer. Certainly it is at the heart of the storyteller's art. Sense of timing can be improved by experimenting with the rhythm and pace of story delivery.

■ After hearing a story retell it rapidly to a succession of partners. Try the 30 second version a few times before graduating to the two, or five, minute version. Try chanting it, singing it, calling it, whispering it all with varying degrees of urgency.

■ Tell the story's climax as if it was a commentary on a sporting event like horse racing or football. It is building the underlying tension that is important, not necessarily the speed of delivery.

■ In telling a story become aware of where you want to pause, but feel that if you do you'll lose your audience. Try exaggerating your pauses in those places. Then introduce pauses in unexpected places, and continue on flowingly where you might normally stop.

Telling and Re-telling Stories There is nothing rote or uncreative about retelling a story. It is a challenging and original oral art. Children often exceed their normal language levels in retelling a story.

■ Tell a story to a class and then ask them to tell it back, either in pairs or in

Chysauster Ancient Village, Cornwall.

small groups. If one person forgets someone else will probably remember and almost the whole story will be recalled.

■ Once you've told a story a few times record yourself telling it onto a tape. Listen to the playback. Don't judge yourself too harshly but use it to discover ways in which you might improve your telling.

■ Children prepare a story and then tell it to younger children in other classes. This involves careful selection of material and working out how to adapt the telling appropriately.

■ Spread a story through the school...!

Kathie Prince telling Raven brings the daylight at Avebury, Wiltshire.

Let's go back in time

ERIC MADDERN

© 1990 Eric Maddern

TIME-TRAVEL SONG

Let's go back in time

Chorus
Let's go back in time
One hundred(1), two hundred,
three hundred years
To the time of the earliest
people living here
Four hundred, five hundred,
six hundred years.
Let's go back in time
To the time of our
grandfathers' (2),
grandfathers', grandfathers',
grandfathers (3) …
grandfathers', grandfather.

Walking through the ruins of
this old, old place
Let your mind wander back in
time
Imagine what was happening
when it was alive
Can you see the pictures in
your mind?

High on a windy hilltop
(repeat each line as 'call and
response')
Maiden Castle stands
Circled by great ramparts
It overlooks the land
The home of Celtic chieftains
A place for storing grain
They lived here five hundred
years
Till the Roman army came

Chorus

(1) Can be 'hundreds' or
'thousands' depending on age
of site

(2) Can be 'grandfathers' or
'grandmothers' or alternated

(3) Sing 10 or 12 times or
according to time to be
travelled

Singing 'Let's go
back in time' at Old
Sarum.

RESOURCES AND BIBLIOGRAPHY

In this selected bibliography the books containing stories from the oral tradition have been placed according to whether their major emphasis is myth, legend or folktale. Some books defy such classification and could be included in almost any category.

MYTH

Campbell, Joseph **The Masks of God** 4 vols, Esp Vol 1. **Primitive Mythology** and Vol 3. **Occidental Mythology.** Penguin 1969 ISBN 0-1400-4304-7 also **The Hero with a Thousand faces,** Paladin 1975 ISBN 0-586-08571-8

Colom, Padraic **Orpheus: Myths of the World** Floris Classics 1991 ISBN 0-86315-519-7

Frazer, James **The Golden Bough: A Study in Magic and Religion** Papermac 1987 (abridged edition) ISBN 0-333-52198-6

Gersic, Alida **Earthtales: Storytelling in Times of Change** Green Print 1992 ISBN 1-85425-065-5

Graves, Robert (Intro) **New Larousse Encyclopedia of Mythology** Hamlyn 1989 ISBN 0-600-2350-8

Haviland, Virginia **North American Legends** Faber 1979 ISBN 0-571-13167-0

Parabola: **The Magazine of Myth and Tradition** (from Parabola, 656 Broadway, New York, N.Y. 10012-9824) ISSN 0362-1596

Rosenberg, Donna **World Mythology: An Anthology of the Great Myths and Epics** Harrap 1986 ISBN 0-245-54493-3

Sproul, Barbara **Primal Myths** Harper & Row 1979 ISBN 0-06-067501-2

Travers, P.L. **What the Bee Knows: Reflections on Myth, Symbol and Story** Aquarian Press 1989 ISBN 0-85030-786-4

LEGEND

Ashe, Geoffrey **Mythology of the British Isles** Methuen 1990 ISBN 0-413-62290-2

Bede **The Ecclesiastical History of the English People** Penguin 1990 ISBN 0-14-044565-X

Chant, Joy **The High Kings: Arthur's Celtic Ancestors** George Allen and Unwin 1983 ISBN 0-04-823240-8

Crossley-Holland, Kevin **The Norse Myths** Pantheon 1981 ISBN 0-23-39727-4

Geoffrey of Monmouth **History of the Kings of Britain** trans. Lewis Thorpe Penguin 1968 ISBN 0-14-044170-0

Gregory, Lady **Gods and Fighting Men** Colin Smythe Pbk ed, 1976 ISBN 0-901072-37-0

Harrison, Michael **The Doom of the Gods** OUP 1985 ISBN 0-19-274128-4

Jones, Gwyn & Jones, Thomas **The Mabinogion** Everyman's Library 1949/1986 ISBN 0-460-11097-7

Jones, Gwyn **Welsh Legends and Folk Tales** Puffin/OUP 1955/1979 ISBN 0-14-031097-5

Matthews, Caitlin **The Celtin Tradition** Element 1989 ISBN 1-85230-075-2

Matthews, John **The Arthurian Tradition** Element 1989 ISBN 1-85230-074-4

Middleton, Haydn **The Island of the Mighty** OUP 1987 ISBN 0-19-274133-0

Rees, Alwyn and Brinley **Celtic Heritage: Ancient Tradition in Ireland and Wales** Thames and Hudson 1961 ISBN 0-500-11008-5

Rolleston, T.W. **Myths and Legends of the Celtic Race** Constable 1985 ISBN 0-09-467720-4

Ross, Anne **Druids Gods and Heroes from Celtic Mythology** Peter Lowe 1986 ISBN 0-95210-232-2

Ross, Anne & Robins, Don **The Life and Death of a Druid Prince: The Story of an Archaeological Sensation** Rider 1989 ISBN 0-7126-2511-9

Rutherford, Ward **Celtic Mythology: The Nature and Influence of Celtic Myth from Druidism to Arthurian Legend** Aquarian Press 1987

ISBN 0-85030-551-9

Snelling, John **Celtic Myths and Legends** Wayland 1988 ISBN 1-85210-232-2

Thomas, Gwyn & Crossley-Holland, Kevin **The Quest for Olwen** Lutterworth Press ISBN 0-7188-2706-6

Williamson, Robin **The Craneskin Bag** Canongate 1989 ISBN 0-86241-218-8

Young, Ella **Celtic Wondertales** Floris Clasics 1988 ISBN 0-86315-510-3

FOLK AND FAIRY TALES

Adams, Richard **Grimm's Fairy Tales** Routledge & Kegan Paul 1983 ISBN 0-7100-9997-5

Alexander, Marc **British Folklore, Myths and Legends** George Weidenfeld & Nicolson 1982 ISBN 0-297-78151-0

Briggs, Katherine & Tongue, Ruth L **Folktales of England** Routledge & Kegan Paul 1965 ISBN 7-100-6680-5

Briggs, Katherine **A Dictionary of British Folk Tales in the English Language; Part A Folk Narrative, Part B Folk Legends** Routledge 1991 ISBN Pt A 0-415-06694-8 Pt B 0-415-06695-6

Carter, Angela **The Virago Book of Fairy Tales** Virago 1990 ISBSN 1-85381-205-6

Crossley-Holland, Kevin **Folk Tales of the British Isles** Faber 1985 ISBN 0-571-13786-5

Crossley-Holland, Kevin **British and Irish Folk Tales: a Selection of Stories from British Folk Tales** Orchard 1987 ISBN 1-85213-265-5

Garner, Alan **Book of British Fairy Tales** Collins 1984 ISBN 0-00-184048-7

Glassie, Henry **Irish Folk Tales** Penguin Folklore Library 1987 ISBN 0-14-059509-0

Jacobs, Joseph **English Fairy Tales** The Bodley Head 1984 ISBN 0-370-01023-X

Jacobs, Joseph **Celtic Fairy Tales** The Bodley Head 1985 ISBN 0-370-30682-1

Marshall, Sybil **Everyman's Book of English Folk Tales** Everyman Classics 1985 ISBN 0-460-01497-8

O'Faolain, Eileen **Irish Sagas and Folk Tales** Poolbeg 1986 ISBN 0-905169-71-9

Williamson, Duncan and Linda **A Thorn in the King's Foot: Stories of the Scottish Travelling People** Penguin Folklore library 1987 ISBN 0-14-059508-2

Williamson, Duncan **Fireside Tales of the Traveller Children** Canongate 1983 ISBN 0-86241-100-9

Williamson, Duncan **Don't Look Back, Jack!** Canongate 1990 ISBN 0-86241-309-5

In addition to these works there are many collections of folktales or yarns which relate to specific regions or counties. They can be a useful source of local tales.

HISTORICAL NOVELS

The two outstanding historical novelists for young people are Henry Treece and Rosemary Sutcliffe. Their works include:

Sutcliffe, Rosemary **Sun Horse, Moon Horse** Knight 1977 ISBN 0-340-26815-8

Song for a Dark Queen Pelham 1978 ISBN 0-7207-1060-X

Dragon Slayer: Story of Beowulf Puffin ISBN 0-14-030254-9

The High Deeds of Finn MacCool Puffin ISBN B-682-538-6

The Light Beyond the Forest Knight 1979 ISBN 0-340-25821-7

The Chronicles of Robin Hood OUP ISBN 791-0369-6

Treece, Henry **Legions of the Eagle** Puffin 1965 ISBN 0-14-030247-6

Hounds of the King Bodley Head 1971 ISBN 0-370-0221-6

Last of the Vikings Beaverbrooks 1976 ISBN 0-600-35509-8

Morris, Margery **Stories of the Ancient Britons** Severn House 1977 ISBN 0-7278-0292-5

ARTHURIAN LEGEND

Over the centuries there have been hundreds of works of fiction inspired by Arthurian and related legends.

Bradley, Marion **The Mists of Avalon** Sphere Books 1982 ISBN 0-7221-1957-7

Sampson, Fay **Wise Woman's Telling** Headline 1989 ISBN 0-7472-3263-6

Stewart, Mary **The Crystal Cave** Hodder & Stoughton/Coronet 1970 ISBN 0-340-15133-1

von Strasburg, Gottfired **Tristan** Penguin Classics 1967 ISBN 0-14-044098-4

White, T.H. **Once and Future King** Collins 1958 ISBN 0-0002-21601-9

ABOUT STORYTELLING

Channel 4 TV **By Word of Mouth: The Revival of Storytelling** 1989 Copies at 3.00 from By Word of Mouth, Channel 4 TV, PO Box 400, London W3 6XJ

Colwell, Eileen **Storytelling** The Bodley Head 1980 ISBN 0-370-30228-1

Gersie, A & King, N **Storymaking in Education and Therapy** Jessica Kingsley 1990 ISBN 1-85302-520-8

Rosen, Betty **And None of It Was Nonsense: The Power of Storytelling in School** Mary Glasgow 1988 ISBN 1-85234-191-2

Rosen, Michael **Did I Hear You Write!** Andrew Deutsch 1989 ISBN 0-233-98381-3

Sawyer, Ruth **The Way of the Storyteller** Viking ISBN 0-370-01082-5

RESOURCES

Since the early 1980's a revival of storytelling has been gathering pace in Britain. For information about storytelling events contact:

The Crick Crack Club, c/o Interchange Studios, Dalby St, London NW5 3NQ. Tel: 071 284 4367

There is a growing band of modern storytellers who work in schools, libraries, festivals, clubs, museum and historic sites. Information about them is in The Directory of Storytellers which can be obtained from:

The Children's Book Foundation, 45 East Hill, Wandsworth, London SW18 2QY

Facts and Fiction is a quarterly storytelling newsletter containing information on storytelling. It is available from: Facts and Fiction, 6 Fleur Gates, Princes Way, London SW19.

CIRCLE DANCES

Tapes and instructions on circle dances for children and adults are available from: Dancing Circles, PO Box 26,

Glastonbury, Somerset BA6 9YA (Tel: 0278 786307).

STORYTELLING TAPES

The Company of Storytellers. Available from: The Company of Storyteller's Tapes, c/o 8 Church Terrace, Aylsham, Norfolk NR11 6EU.

Eric Maddern, Storytelling at Historic Sites. A selection of Myths, Legends and Folktales selected, adapted and told by Eric Maddern with musical accompaniment. 2 × 90 minute cassettes; 1992. Price £9.95. Available from English Heritage, PO Box 229, Northampton NN6 9RY.

Robin Williamson. Information and tapes available from: Robin Williamson Production. BCM Box 4797, London WC1N 3XX.

Taffy Thomas. Available from: Taffy Thomas, Beech Cottage, Grassmere, Cumbria LA22 9SU.

Tim Bowley. Available from: Tim Bowley, 2 Castle St, Newcastle Emlyn, Dyfed SA38 0AG.

ACKNOWLEDGEMENTS

Thanks especially to Kathie Prince and Hugh Lupton and also to Martin Gill, Tim Bowley, Linda Cotterill, Duncan Williamson, Mary Medlicott and Ben Haggarty.